HOME STYLE

YourHome

HOME STYLE

CHOOSE AND CREATE THE LOOK THAT'S RIGHT FOR YOU AND YOUR HOME

Kerryn Harper

hamlyn

First published in Great Britain in 2002
by Hamlyn, a division of Octopus Publishing
Group Limited
2–4 Heron Quays, London E14 4JP

Originally published as *Home: A Practical
Style Guide*
This edition published in 2005

ISBN 0 600 61208 2
EAN 9780600612087

A CIP catalogue record for this book is
available from the British Library

Printed and bound in China

10 9 8 7 6 5 4 3 2 1

CONTENTS

INTRODUCTION

CHOOSING YOUR LOOK

Decorating your home should be a fulfilling and exciting experience, but all too often homeowners fall at the very first hurdle, unable to decide what sort of style and mood they are trying to create. So if you have ever found yourself struggling to choose a colour scheme, or you have a rough idea of the look you are after but are not quite sure how to pull a whole room together, this is the book for you.

Packed with inspirational photography, *Home – a Practical Style Guide* gives you comprehensive step-by-step advice on how to choose every ingredient of the ten most popular decorating styles. It is not about keeping up with fashion or about learning how to become a professional designer; it is about enjoying making the most of your home and decorating to suit yourself. I guarantee that it will help reduce the heartache of indecision and make decorating a real pleasure. So stop worrying about the rules, take a risk and experiment. The feel-good factor that comes from creating a new room scheme that you really love will repay your time and effort over and over again.

▸ **With its sophisticated colour schemes and muted fabrics, elegant French chic looks harder to put together than it actually is.**

three things to consider before you search for your look

▲ **Consider your lifestyle carefully before opting for a gorgeous minimalist cream scheme if you want a room that will stay looking good.**

be **realistic** about your lifestyle

Tastes in interior design come and go, so the most fundamental question to ask yourself when choosing a new room scheme is whether or not it is really practical for your day-to-day life. You may love the idea of a minimalist open-plan apartment, but if you have a family, the reality of living with no dividing walls to stop noise travelling and slow the inevitable spread of clutter should make you think again. Equally, if you spend long hours at work and are rarely at home, you have to acknowledge the fact that you need a low-maintenance style, which is not going to take lots of primping and preening to stay looking good. Thinking of

owning a dog or a cat? Then forget your dreams of that to-die-for cream sofa. Stain-resistant, scratch-proof furniture and easy-clean flooring are your new must-buys. Expecting a baby? Then you can rule out glass-topped tables (breakable), sharp-cornered furniture, strip-metal kitchen handles (especially at child-head height) and natural-textured floorings (think of the friction burns on crawling knees). Being practical when you choose a décor style means not only that you will love your new look but that you can actually live with it, too. This book offers lots of suggestions on how to interpret a style so as to tailor it to your own needs.

Your home is the one space you control, which
makes it the ideal place to express yourself, decorating
rooms to suit your particular tastes. So if you want to
create somewhere you can really feel at home in, forget
what the fashion gurus tell you and be honest about
your character. Introverts might consider pepping
themselves up by using exuberant décor, when in
actual fact they would simply feel ill at ease with the
end results. Similarly, extroverts may stare wistfully at
classy white-on-white schemes in magazines, but in
reality would find all that neutrality boring and bland in
no time. It is always better to be true to yourself and
play to your strengths. After all, your rooms should
flatter you as much as you would expect a well-chosen
outfit to do. Of course, if you live with other people you
may have to compromise in order to ensure that no one
feels overwhelmed by your choices, but negotiating
and inspiring new ideas in each other often produces
the most interesting end results.

be **true** to your personality

▸ **Bold Moroccan shades
suit extrovert personalities
and homes of those who
love to entertain.**

▸ Restoring period details, such as cornicing and picture rails, to an older property can add value and renew its charm but can look totally out of keeping in a modern, lower ceiling home.

choose décor to **complement** the style and period of your property

You do not have to decorate a warehouse conversion in loft style or a seaside house with a nautical theme, but you would be wise to aim for décor that has something in harmony with the age and location of your home. The proportions of your rooms, the number of windows you have and even the direction your windows face should all also influence the choices you make. Modern standard-height rooms, for example, look twee and feel claustrophobic with ornate Victorian coving, dados and so on, which only make the rooms

feel smaller. North-facing homes receive a cold bluish daylight, which can make pastel shades look positively icy and unwelcoming. South-facing homes with yellow daylight can make warm, rich shades look garish instead of creating the bold sunshine feel you were hoping for. So take time to use those tester pots of paint and live with swatches of colour on the wall for at least a week to be sure. It is amazing how colours can change at different times of the day and in different rooms. Your patience will be rewarded.

HOW TO USE THIS BOOK

▲ Inspiration for a new room scheme can come from a favourite group of colours, a single accessory or even a holiday abroad. This tranquil scheme was inspired by a stay in an oriental hotel.

Finding inspiration for a new room scheme is the biggest problem for many decorators, but it can be as simple as starting with a flower colour you particularly love or a decorating style you have seen on holiday which has a mood and feel you would like to try and recapture at home. To help you on your way, I have put together chapters on the ten most popular decorating styles, complete with step-by-step guides on how to blend all the essential ingredients. There is something here for all tastes and lifestyles – all you have to do is

decide which one appeals to you the most. Just remember that the aim of this book is to inspire you rather than dictate a fashionable look for your home. You will not find any absolute decorating formulas here, but instead a number of easy-to-follow guidelines to get you started and help you succeed. Feel free to interpret the styles and adapt them to suit your requirements, and never be intimidated into thinking there is a right or a wrong look. However loosely you follow these suggestions, you are sure to love the end results.

take the **taste** challenge

To begin, turn to page 18 and use the flow chart to help you find a style that suits you. Just answer the questions as honestly as you can and the chart will lead you to one or two styles that should fit your needs. Many of the looks featured have a number of qualities in common, so if you want greater flexibility, finish at the penultimate stage of the chart and consider two or more looks instead of honing your choice down to one straightaway.

Another option is to turn directly to the colour palettes at the beginning of each chapter and gauge your responses to them. If you like cool, dreamy hues, some schemes will instantly jump off the page at you, and the same is true if you prefer hot, dramatic or cosy looks. You will intuitively find yourself gravitating towards specific chapters and the decorating style which will make you feel most at home.

Choosing by colour palette can lead to surprising new décor ideas that are well worth experimenting with. Tropical ethnic style and traditional English, for example, have many of the same key characteristics (dark wood, cosy clutter, tiled floors and so on), so be careful not to dismiss a look simply because of any preconceived ideas you might have. Experimenting is half the fun, so remember that you can always use the basic colour palette and then pick and choose how authentic you want to be through your choice of furniture and accessories, giving the flavour of a particular style rather than going for the whole theme in every room.

▸ **Style is a very personal thing, so don't be afraid to mix old and new for a look that appeals to your own taste. This delightful bathroom blends an angular 1930s retro suite with modern chrome and mosaic tiles for a period twist in a loft apartment.**

take the **lifestyle** challenge

Once you have decided to focus on two, three or even four chapters that interest you, it is time to use our handy pros and cons boxes within the relevant sections to see if the looks suit your lifestyle. Here again, you need to read the statements and see whether more pros ring true than cons. If so, it is safe to assume that this look will be practical for your home. However, if there are more cons than pros, you need to think hard about whether your dream décor is simply that – an unworkable 'idealistic' image that will simply not cope with the daily rigours of your home and family life.

starting to **compile** the look

Now you have your basic style and mood in mind, it is time to get down to selecting the basic ingredients. Each chapter is packed with practical advice and inspiring ideas for choosing the perfect floors, walls and soft furnishing fabrics for the look. Some are truly authentic while others are a cheat's version for when you prefer to soften the theme to suit, say, the climate or your personal taste.

choosing colour

The eye-catching colour palettes in each chapter give clear guidance on which shades to use for walls, floors, paint, fabrics and even painted furniture around your home. They are not definitive by any means, but will give you a good feel for the sort of tones and colour densities to opt for, and there are more than enough to choose from in order to give each room a completely different look. Many DIY superstores now offer paint-mixing services, so if you are unable to find the colour you are looking for, you could always take this book into

the shop with you and ask someone to scan your choice with a magic eye to produce a perfectly colour-coordinated pot of paint.

Just remember though the colour you see on a small swatch in a chart will appear darker and more intense by the time you have applied it all over the walls, so to play safe you could always choose a colour one or two shades lighter than the one you think you actually want. Do not go for a pastel version of a bold shade, though, as you will only be disappointed. If, however, you are going to use the colour in only smaller doses, for example for curtains or sofa upholstery, it is fine to use any swatch as a direct match. Tester pots of paint and wallpaper swatches are worth the time and effort. Paint at least two sheets of A4 paper or bigger in your chosen colour (same size for wallpaper, too) and then affix them temporarily to two walls in the room you want to decorate. View them over a few days, preferably for at least a week, in all the different lighting conditions you can imagine. What looks gorgeous in daylight may become garish under the yellow-toned bulb of your lights at night; or a colour which looks fresh in the morning may appear grey and sludgy at dusk. This is the best way I know to avoid error and, even though you may feel you are wasting time, I cannot recommend it highly enough.

▼ **Your choice of colour has a huge impact on the mood of any room. Here one vibrant cobalt blue wall totally transforms an otherwise all-white scheme.**

◀ Treat your floor as a fifth wall. Decide whether you want it to add impact or to simply create a neutral backdrop to the rest of your scheme.

▶ Decorating walls is not simply about choosing colour, it's about creating another layer of texture to bring a room to life. Choose the texture to match the mood of your room. Soft sheen and matt emulsions are ideal for elegant, sophisticated rooms, while rough plaster or tongue-and-groove panelling create an instant rustic feel.

▶ Beaded fabrics used even in only small doses can add opulence at minimal cost.

choosing flooring

Climate and location have a huge impact on the choice of flooring each nation prefers for its homes. The British are fonder of carpet than almost any other nation and believe it represents quality and luxury underfoot. Other Europeans prefer a mix of tiles and wooden flooring for practicality, and these are also more hygienic in many cases. When you consider the hotter temperatures of the Mediterranean, for example, it soon becomes apparent why a cool surface is preferable. Tropical countries favour low-maintenance, easy-clean flooring, so as to cope with hot and humid conditions, making sweepable stone floors and rugs that can be beaten free of dust very popular. In every chapter you will find at least four flooring options, with suggestions on how to adapt the authentic choices to your own needs, and on how to cheat with flooring that is not really what it seems.

choosing wall finishes

Colour and texture are always going to be the key considerations here. Rustic looks, for example, require rough plaster and textured finishes, which you may not want to commit yourself to, but if your home already has bumpy or uneven walls, these could be turned to your advantage. There are any number of different ways to fake texture and this book will show you how to adapt them for use in your chosen scheme. Smooth silk or matt paint finishes can offer a more sophisticated, elegant finish but are, of course, prone to showing dirty marks, making them higher maintenance in a family home. You need not restrict yourself to paint and wallpaper, though, when trying to create a totally new look for your home. Wood panelling, tongue-and-groove boarding and even bare brick are all possibilities. The only limit is your attitude to what can be achieved.

choosing fabrics

Soft furnishings can be plain and simple or lavish and opulent. The important thing is to make sure the weight, style and colour of the fabrics you choose match the requirements of your particular scheme. Each chapter will give you all the information you need on the key fabric types and textures to look for, thus taking the fear out of choosing. As a guide to help you shop, there are also fabric swatches to illustrate the sort of patterns that fit each scheme.

Oriental style

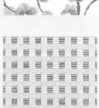

Loft style

creating a mood board

Take a tip from professional interior designers and have a go at compiling your own mini swatch board of fabric samples and paint swatches you fall in love with so you can build up your perfect look. Pin them on a cork board in swatch sizes that relate to the importance of the fabric or paint within the room scheme. For example, a fabric swatch you think is ideal for curtains should be slightly bigger than one used for a sofa, while a paint swatch for your walls should cover at least three times as much space again. This way you will build up an accurate colour balance of all the furnishings in the room. Do not worry too much about trying to match patterns immediately – just pin things together and see how they work. Often, two patterns you assume would look hideous together can complement each other surprisingly well. You can try pinning up flooring samples, too.

▲ **Use inspirational room schemes taken from brochures and magazines as well as details, such as accessories, and fabric and colour swatches, in your mood board to give you an overall feel for a particular style.**

American country style

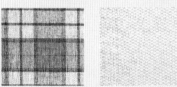

down to the
nitty-gritty

Once your colour scheme is pretty much there and you have found the perfect flooring and fabrics, it is time to focus on the essential ingredients for every room to complete the look. Each chapter gives you guidelines for furniture and accessories to build up your dream kitchen, living room, bedroom and bathroom. If you want a totally authentic and foolproof end result, choose all the ingredients listed and use our colour palette. More confident decorators can simply pick and choose from each list of ingredients to capture the basic feel.

get ready
to **shop**

To complete a clear picture of exactly what you want your room to look like, take just a little longer to research pictures of furniture, accessories and window treatments in magazines and mail-order catalogues. Cut them out and pin them to your mood board as a final double check. Then comes the really fun part: putting it all together. You can obviously work quickly, if time and budget allow, but I think it is worth remembering that decorating and making a home are best treated as an ongoing process. Things done in a rush can look too perfect and too much like a show home, when what you are really trying to create is a place in which you feel comfortable and relaxed rather than perfect but sterile. Building a look slowly allows time for your tastes to develop and stops you from making decisions you might later regret. Every new look should give your home personality and individuality, making the end result totally true to you.

Happy decorating!

find your perfect **home style**

Home fashion trends may come and go, but some styles never date. Find your favourite and narrow down the looks that will suit your taste best of all with this handy flow chart.

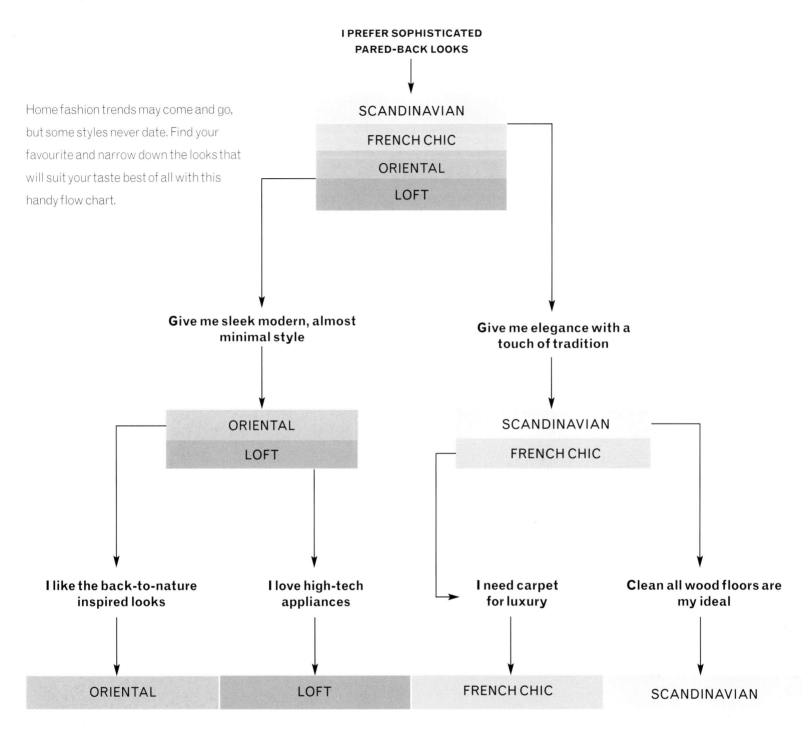

I PREFER SOPHISTICATED PARED-BACK LOOKS

SCANDINAVIAN
FRENCH CHIC
ORIENTAL
LOFT

Give me sleek modern, almost minimal style

ORIENTAL
LOFT

Give me elegance with a touch of tradition

SCANDINAVIAN
FRENCH CHIC

I like the back-to-nature inspired looks

I love high-tech appliances

I need carpet for luxury

Clean all wood floors are my ideal

ORIENTAL

LOFT

FRENCH CHIC

SCANDINAVIAN

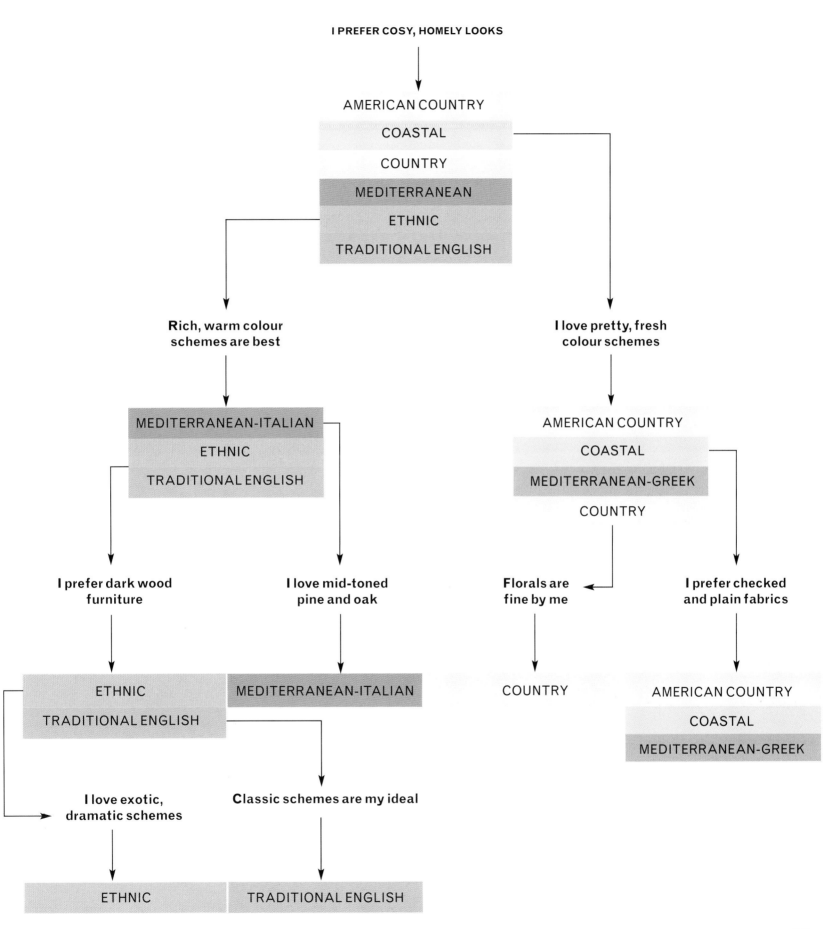

I PREFER COSY, HOMELY LOOKS

AMERICAN COUNTRY
COASTAL
COUNTRY
MEDITERRANEAN
ETHNIC
TRADITIONAL ENGLISH

Rich, warm colour schemes are best

I love pretty, fresh colour schemes

MEDITERRANEAN-ITALIAN
ETHNIC
TRADITIONAL ENGLISH

AMERICAN COUNTRY
COASTAL
MEDITERRANEAN-GREEK
COUNTRY

I prefer dark wood furniture

I love mid-toned pine and oak

Florals are fine by me

I prefer checked and plain fabrics

ETHNIC
TRADITIONAL ENGLISH

MEDITERRANEAN-ITALIAN

COUNTRY

AMERICAN COUNTRY
COASTAL
MEDITERRANEAN-GREEK

I love exotic, dramatic schemes

Classic schemes are my ideal

ETHNIC

TRADITIONAL ENGLISH

TRADITIONAL ENGLISH STYLE

1

TRADITIONAL ENGLISH STYLE

If your taste is for classic décor with charm, character and a touch of opulence, then this style could well be for you. This chapter draws upon general features of different English period homes to help you create a heritage look in keeping with your modern lifestyle.

▾ Gilded accessories, such as this glamorous mirror, and lots of chintzy pattern on cushions and curtains give this opulent living room its traditional feel. Swag window treatments are a common choice, but these can be overwhelming in a lower-ceilinged room.

The interpretation of traditional English style combines flavours from different historical periods that have become classics over the years. It is about creating timeless, elegant yet cosy looks for the average home, not grand schemes suited to a country estate. Dark wood furniture in rich mahogany, walnut or aged oak is your essential starting point and blends beautifully with the warming tones of the colour palette for walls and soft furnishings. Carpet is the most common choice for floors to emphasize the opulent feel of this scheme and is generally used throughout main living and sleeping areas. Classic chequerboard tiles and rich wood or parquet flooring are authentic for halls and kitchens. Brass or gilded accessories, from picture frames to candlestick-style lamp bases and even light switches, add the perfect finishing touches. The golden glow of this metal suiting the colour palette far better than any other choice.

▲ A brass bedstead with globe finials epitomizes this style, combining cosiness and elegance. An open fire in a bedroom is authentic, but you could fake the look with a decorated mantelpiece. The floor-to-ceiling bookcases add a sense of age and can work in any room.

▶ Traditional style need not be dark or terribly formal, as this scheme shows. Here the essential upholstered footstool, dark wood furniture and scroll-armed seating are given a softer take with a variety of patterned fabrics in warm golds, russets and greens.

key characteristics

- **Comfortable carpeting underfoot** in opulent plains and dramatic patterns in main reception rooms.

- **Open fires** or wood-burning stoves with ornate gilt-framed mirrors above a wood, limestone or marble carved mantelpiece.

- **Atmospheric lighting**, including chandeliers, wall-mounted lights with two arms and shaded bulbs, and floor-standing lamps.

- **Brass and crystal accessories**, from picture frames to candlestick-base table lamps.

- **Dark wood furniture**, such as mahogany, redwood and antique oak, with ornate turned legs.

- **Striking window treatments**, including tasselled tiebacks and swagged pelmets plus inset cushioned windowseats.

- **Richly coloured fabrics** in intricate patterns or luxurious textures, such as velvet, chenille, damask and leather.

- **Patterned tiled floors** or wooden marquetry floors in halls and kitchens.

is this **the right look** for me?

Traditional English style is ideal for you if you:
- ✔ yearn for the character and charm of **classic interiors**
- ✔ prefer **inherited furniture** and junk-shop buys
- ✔ love the warmth of **rich dark woods** like mahogany and oak
- ✔ live in a **period property**
- ✔ want to create a cosy yet **elegant** home

Avoid if any of the following is true:
- ✘ **Rich colour schemes** make me feel claustrophobic
- ✘ **Patterned fabrics** are banned from my rooms
- ✘ I live in a **modern** apartment
- ✘ I prefer **light and airy** schemes
- ✘ I find details like dados and **picture rails** too fussy for my taste

COLOUR

Faded grandeur is the phrase that best sums up the broad variety of tones in the traditional English colour palette. The shades bring a surprising combination of drama and comfort to any room. At the deeper end of the colour choice, the rich yet cosy tones of russet, mustard, wine and deep green are ideal for giving character and a subtle glow to rooms that lack natural light. The paler colours – ivory, cream, gold and sage – are perfect for light yet ornate schemes in rooms where you want a more opulent and formal feel.

• Think **Persian rug tones**

TONES LIKE:

ivory
cream
gold
russet
deep rose
heather
pea green
sage
grey-blue
woad
bullrush

TEAM WITH:

- **dressy window treatments such as pelmets, tiebacks or swag tops (not necessarily all three together)**
- **dark woods and brass or gilded accessories**
- **rich carpeting underfoot**

colour tips

If you want to be true to a particular period of English decorating history take a visit to an interior museum to find out the perfect colour palette for any era, or seek out specialist paint and wallpaper manufacturers who have created ranges according to archive material. Georgian and Victorian themes are the ones that most often spring to mind when we talk of traditional English design, although there is no reason to follow the palette slavishly unless you wish to be absolutely authentic in the restoration of a period property. Our main palette takes inspiration from both periods but predominantly the Victorian era for its warmer and arguably richer shades.

GEORGIAN STYLE 1714–1837

Walls would have been painted in a single colour, with either white paint or occasionally a darker shade used to emphasize detailing on skirtings, doors and panelling. Colour choice often depended on the aspect of the room, with **warm pale pinks**, **golds** and **lemons** used for north-facing rooms and **sky blues** and **deeper greens**, such as **pea green**, used in southerly settings with **white** ceilings— **off-white** rather than brilliant white in today's terms—for both.

VICTORIAN STYLE 1837–1901

The Victorian palette is dominated by **warm terracotta** shades, which made the perfect contrast to terracotta-tiled floors and multi-coloured brickwork of the period. Three-part colour schemes were popular with a different shade used from floor to dado, then dado to picture rail and finally picture rail to ceiling, although below dado was often decorated with embossed paper rather than paint.

WALLS

Think long and hard before you start decorating your walls because in this scheme the walls are dramatic features in their own right. From heavily patterned wallpaper to panelling to rich matt paints, there is plenty of choice for adding character and playing with different moods.

Bold paint shades, heavily patterned wallpapers and strong textured finishes, such as tiling and panelling, are all good choices, but since they could also easily be overwhelming you need to make sure that they will blend in with the rest of your look rather than dominate. Georgian homes often featured walls panelled from floor to ceiling, which would have been painted in a single colour. Elaborate plaster mouldings, including ceiling roses, were very popular. Victorian walls were commonly split into three, with wallpaper up to dado rail at about one-third wall height, toning matt-finish paint to picture rail height and a paler tone between the picture rail and the ceiling itself. Victorian and Georgian properties had larger rooms and higher ceilings than modern houses, so copying the look to perfection is best avoided except in authentic period homes. For the average property take inspiration from the colours and themes without going overboard for an authentic look. Bold matt-finish or eggshell paints work well – particularly in warming or creamy shades.

◀ **Panelled walls add instant character and an air of history. D**ark wood panelling is authentic but can look heavy and overpowering, so it usually works well only in very large rooms that can afford to feel a little smaller. **There is, however, an exception to this rule: in tiny rooms, such as a study, where no amount of decoration will make the room feel larger, dark wood panelling can add atmosphere. Painted panelling, on the other hand, is easier to work into the average home and looks particularly good in a hallway up to dado height, for example, or as a focus wall in a bedroom or dining room.**

▲ **Plain painted walls are perfectly in keeping, too, and you can use either matt or eggshell finishes for the most authentic end result. Matt paints appear to intensify the tone of the colour applied and look particularly good with deep reds, golds and pea greens for a traditional look. Woodwork should always have a glossy eggshell finish.**

▾ Decorative plaster mouldings such as cornicing, dados and picture rails all contribute to a traditional feel but need to be used with care. Adding such details to modern homes can look false and a little pretentious unless the room proportions are similar to period properties. Choose mouldings to match the age of your home – ornately carved designs will suit older properties, while simply curved cornicing will work better in a modern home.

▲ Wallpaper is a wonderful way to add cosiness and can hide a multitude of sins such as bumpy walls. Concentrate on strongly traditional motifs, such as large chintz floral prints, tiny but densely regular motifs like fleur-de-lis, self-patterned damask finishes where the pattern is picked out only by a sheen from the matt background, and ultra-classic stripes – both thick and pinstripe work well. The dense leaf paper shown is inspired by a William Morris original.

◀ Embossed wallcoverings were a favourite feature of the Victorians who liked to use them as ornate decoration up to dado height. Here an embossed blown vinyl border is used to create relief at picture rail height for an instant period flavour.

FLOORS

Treating your floor as a fifth wall rather than as a subtle base for your room scheme is the key to success when choosing a traditional floor-covering. Pattern and texture are essential – from ornately floral Wilton-style carpeting to painstakingly laid patterns in tiled floors.

Thickly textured quality carpets suit this look better than anything else, although wall-to-wall carpet itself is a relatively modern invention. The Victorians laid huge carpet rugs showing just a narrow border of the wood-blocked flooring. They used tiles in halls, bathrooms and kitchens for practicality. Intricate patterns featuring four or five different coloured tiles were the norm in even the average home, although black and white chequerboard tiles were popular from the early to mid-part of the 20th century.

◀ **O**rnate silk or Persian rugs with a smooth-weave finish can bring pattern and focus to a plain carpet or wooden floor and will instantly imbue a bland scheme with a traditional look. **C**hoose colours that bring together all the other elements of your scheme. This rug, with a rich, dark border and paler patterned centre, is ideal and will not dominate your room.

▲ **N**othing adds warmth and luxury to a room the way carpet does. **In B**ritain it has always been associated with wealth, since originally only the upper classes could afford it. **D**ensely patterned leaf or floral designs and top-quality **A**xminsters, like the one here, are the ideal choice. **C**hoose a cream background if you don't want a full-on colour effect.

▾ **P**arquet is a form of wooden flooring in which blocks are laid to maximize the visual impact made by the wood's grain running in different directions. Genuine parquet is fairly expensive and needs to be fitted professionally, but you can mimic the look with wood-effect laminates or high-quality hard vinyls.

◄ **B**lack and white chequerboard tiled floors are practically a cliché for traditional English style, but as they look so elegant and timeless, and as they work so beautifully in kitchens, bathroom and halls, it is no wonder they continue to be popular. The size of tile you choose will affect the end result. **S**maller squares laid in a diamond pattern, as shown here, suit the narrow confines of a hallway, while larger squares suit similarly large square spaces.

▲ **T**erracotta- and slate-tiled floors are a warmer-looking alternative to black and white tiles and have a strong Victorian feel, reminiscent of original pathways leading to the front doors of older properties. They work beautifully in hallways and rustic-themed kitchens, and you can fake the look with vinyl if you prefer a less hard and noisy finish underfoot.

FABRICS

Pattern is a very important factor when it comes to creating a traditional English setting. The aim is to provide layers of visual interest, so mix a selection of patterns in toning fabrics, such as a stripe teamed with a two-tone floral and a self-patterned plain, all in two or three shades.

Traditional English style has borrowed heavily from décor worldwide. The Georgians loved Grecian and Roman imagery, hence the common use of acanthus leaves in upholstery fabrics. The Victorians were great explorers and loved to echo imagery from their travels abroad, from Turkish and Persian rugs to French rococo styling and Italian Renaissance looks – the more opulent the better. Key fabric designs for a non-specific classical look include two-tone wide striped designs with a narrow stripe highlight in a third

contrasting shade between. Self-patterned damasks in which a single colour fabric is given a three-dimensional effect with matt and shiny areas of relief on the same piece of material offer subtlety for large areas of upholstery. Large paisley prints in rich brick, gold, green and blue tones hint at colonial travels, while large floral chintzes work well in paler schemes featuring such shades as sage, duck-egg blue, gold and cream. In terms of texture, velvets and chenilles make wonderful choices for curtaining.

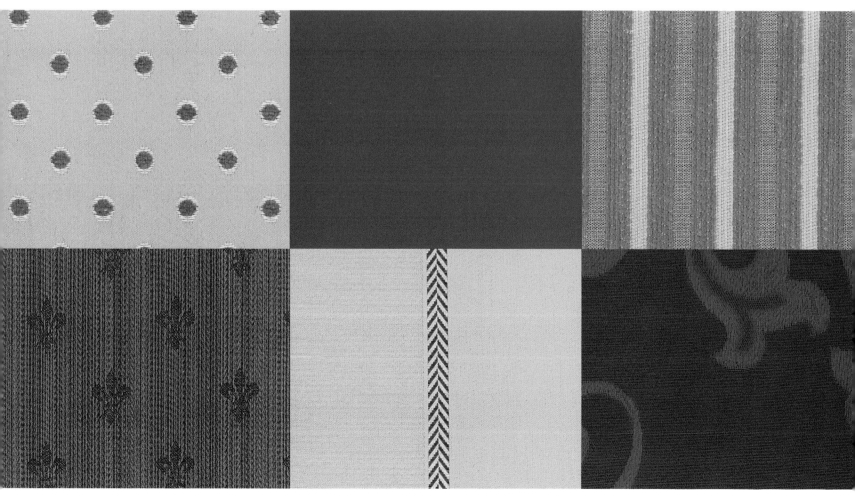

The dramatic paisley print on this eiderdown gives an opulent, slightly colonial feel to the richly coloured bedroom, while the hound's-tooth check reverse adds versatility. A combination of velvet and damask cushions provides subtle contrast to complete the look.

▲ Traditional style need not be all about rich, dark schemes. Placing elegant old golds and sage greens together against a backdrop of cream is a perfectly acceptable alternative as long as you choose traditional patterned accessories, such as damask, striped and floral chintz cushions.

▶ Deeper maroon and gold shades create a rich, cosy living room scheme. Lots of layers of different small-motif patterns on the walls and furniture, together with the bolder curtains, stop the look from becoming too dense and overwhelming.

KITCHEN

One of the most ornate styles for kitchens, this look features heavily moulded units with panelled door fronts in a dark wood or aged paint finishes – ivory with darkened mouldings, for example – and cast-metal handles as a decorative detail in their own right.

Heavily moulded units, commonly with a central, fixed work island with yet more drawers and cupboards means that this scheme works best in larger rooms. To be truly authentic, a range cooker or Aga is the ultimate choice, and, although you can cheat with a fitted oven, it is best to choose a fairly chunky, dominant double-oven design fitted under the counter-top. Modern fittings, such as a stainless steel sink, look completely out of place, so consider instead a ceramic butler's sink or a manmade Corian® alternative. Try to choose concealed appliances, such as dishwashers, fridges and freezers disguised with matching door fronts, to minimize the level of high-tech equipment on display.

kitchen **essentials**

- ✔ ornate **panelled kitchen door fronts** in a dark wood or aged paint effect
- ✔ **cast-metal handles** (pewter tones are ideal)
- ✔ **flagstone**, real wood or tiled flooring
- ✔ **butler's sink**
- ✔ Aga or **range-style** oven
- ✔ wood or **slate-coloured** work-tops
- ✔ **central island** workspace

▸ **Wall-hung plate racks echo traditional English style perfectly,** adding the character that modern wall-to-wall units can sometimes lack. **Look for painted designs with delicately twisted or moulded plate supports for a classic, polished look. Rustic country kitchens feature plate racks, too, but** with simple pine dowelling uprights, which naturally look much less sophisticated.

▲ **An Aga is a big investment but remember that not only will it cook, it can also double as your central heating system.**

▼ **D**etailed moulding on panelled doors and drawers and skirting board-style plinths at the base of the units contribute to the rather ornate look of this kitchen. **C**hoosing a pale painted finish creates a surprisingly light feel that is accentuated by the use of glass panels in some cupboard fronts – not authentic, but visually pleasing. **N**ote how the units combine knob and cage-style handles for interest and mix in wooden work-tops and wicker baskets for texture and contrast. **R**ich dark blue walls add dramatic contrast to complete the traditional-looking scheme.

◀ **W**ooden, slate or granite work-tops are the ideal choices, but here manmade **C**orian® in malachite apes the effect for a low-maintenance alternative, and provides a rich, dark contrast to mid-toned maple units.

▼ **C**hrome mixer-style taps with a swan- or a hooked-neck design as shown give an instant period look to any kitchen. The neat ceramic soap-holder is a charming addition for a **V**ictorian feel and the two-tone tiles create a rustic yet traditional splashback.

LIVING ROOM

An open fireplace is the ultimate focal point for a classic living room. If you do not have the luxury of a chimney or prefer a low-maintenance real flame-effect fire, a gas or electric design can still work well if you choose the design carefully.

A traditional fireplace can be interpreted in many ways, but the two key choices are stone-carved designs and dark wood mantelpieces with inset tiled surrounds. Cast-iron grates add a charming touch, and look out, too , for carved corbel-style mantle supports to give a distinguished finish. Your furniture should offer a combination of subtle grandeur and comfort. Knole sofas with drop-leaf arms suit larger homes, while button-back Chesterfields and scroll-armed sofas with fitted skirt bases are classics that will not dominate the standard-sized room. If you have space for an upholstered footstool with turned legs, this makes a wonderful alternative to a coffee table and is much more in keeping with the look. To finish the scheme, add a console table, a bookcase and sofa side tables, all in rich dark woods, and opulent carpeting or Persian rugs, with a selection of table lamps, floor-standing lamps and wall lights with candle-style shades for a soft atmospheric glow.

▲ This traditional tiled-surround fireplace is given greater presence by the addition of an impressive gilded over-mantel mirror, a common item in the traditional home. **Gold and brass suit this style better than other metals. A** brass fireplace set including poker makes the perfect hearth accessory.

▸ **Single armchairs in non-matching upholstery to your sofa are essential to classic décor. Look for high- or winged-back designs, low arms and wooden turned legs, preferably on brass castors for the perfect complement.**

▲ Table lamps are essential for spreading a warm glow into corners in the traditional home. They add character not only to deep period colour schemes but also where you have opted for pale walls and soft furnishings. Choose cream shades and candlestick bases and gilded or crystal glass ginger jar-shaped bases for the most authentic look.

▲ Rich shades of russet and gold set a cosy mood in this scheme, while the mix of ornate fabrics in subdued tones adds a sense of faded grandeur for a traditional yet relaxed feel. The wood choices are perhaps not as dark as they might be for a truly opulent finish, but this shows how you can interpret the look to create a more subtle and less dominant room setting. Swap this rug for a deep-toned Persian one or a rich-coloured carpet and you will have a near-perfect end result.

living room essentials

- ✔ open or **real flame-effect** fire
- ✔ Chesterfield or **scroll-armed** sofa
- ✔ **winged armchair** or armchair with dark wooden scrolled legs
- ✔ **dark wood** furniture such as a bookcase and chest of drawers
- ✔ **candlestick-based** table lamps
- ✔ rich carpet and **soft rugs** underfoot

BEDROOM

Your choice of bed will help direct the rest of the scheme. The three main options are an ornate brass or wrought-iron bedstead – especially Victorian styles with ball finials on each corner post – and a solid wood bateau-lit design with curved head- and baseboard.

A four-poster bed with turned dark wood posts is another possibility, but only if your room is big enough to take such an imposing feature. Dress the bed with layers of white sheets, blankets, damask bedspreads and even an eiderdown rather than a duvet, which is a very modern concept. For storage, choose a solid-looking, freestanding wardrobe in dark wood such as mahogany, preferably without legs, a dressing table and matching chest of drawers for authenticity. The idea is to choose substantial yet fairly streamlined items that add presence without detracting from the bed. Full-length curtains that 'puddle' on to the carpet create an opulent yet cosy look. You can make a slim window more impressive by fitting a pole slightly wider on either side, allowing for more heavily draped curtains. Cream-shaded table lamps and antique prints finish this elegant look.

bedroom essentials

✔ **brass** or wrought-iron bedstead or solid wood bateau-lit
✔ **damask** bedlinen
✔ **round bedside tables** with fabric tablecloth
✔ **carpeted** flooring
✔ dark wood freestanding wardrobe and **dressing table**
✔ **chandelier** lighting

➤ A rich damask, velvet or chenille throw adds an opulent look to any bed and this particular tasselled design has a rather regal feel, with its swirling acanthus and dolphin imagery in crimson and gold.

➤ This impressive-looking wardrobe is a good reproduction example of a solid period wardrobe, although a three-door design would be the perfect choice.

◄ **Crystal-drop chandeliers** are a wonderful lighting choice for any traditional-style room and add a romantic note to a bedroom. This design mixes coloured glass with clear droplets for a rich and eye-catching look, but a gold coloured and plain crystal design would work equally well.

▼ **A** luxurious-looking solid bateau-lit bed creates an impressive focal point and is elegantly dressed with plain white linen for a crisp contrast to the mahogany tones. The classic gold walls add a rich glow to the scheme, while three botanical prints in gilded frames add drama and symmetry above the bedhead for a formal look. Note the fabric-dressed circular bedside table, which adds a soft touch, and the large cream-shaded table lamp, which is ideal for creating a cosy mood at dusk.

BATHROOM

Period-style sanitary ware is of course the starting point for a classic bathroom, although you do not need to be too pedantic about confining yourself to a particular era. A traditional freestanding roll-top bath with gilded feet in a slipper bath or single end design is ideal.

Gold taps and fittings look regal against deep red walls, while chrome is more suitable for dark green or blue schemes. Some roll-top baths even come with paintable exteriors, so you can colour them either to match or to contrast with the rest of the room. If you do not have the space for a roll-top or prefer a more practical fitted bath, you can still give it a period feel with the addition of a bath/shower handset mixer in place of ordinary pillar taps. A high-level cistern toilet and a basin set into a vanity unit complete the look. When choosing the décor, consider tiled walls to at least dado height, with painted or wallpapered walls above. Tiles on the floor are also an authentic option – particularly in black and white diamond or chequerboard designs. Carpet is acceptable, too, if cosiness is your primary concern.

▶ **Attention to detail gives this bathroom its traditional feel. A slipper bath is given pride of place while gold fittings add an opulent note. Both the black and white chequerboard floor and walls tiled to dado level are authentic for the look. Practical roller blinds are softened with muslin drapes to echo the classical mood.**

bathroom **essentials**

✔ **roll-top** bath
✔ **high-level** cistern toilet
✔ carpet or **tiled flooring**
✔ **period-style bath/shower mixer tap**
✔ sink set into a wooden or **marble-topped vanity unit** or a pedestal basin
✔ curtains or **draped voiles** at the window
✔ freestanding **towel rail** in dark wood

▶ **Shower cubicles are, of course, a modern development, but you can still create a traditional feel by adding an etched-glass door and a rich-tiled interior. The etched motif shown here is one of the most popular 'classic' designs around.**

◀ **Keep** everything close to hand on a chrome or gold-plated bath rack as the perfect permanent accessory for your bath. It makes relaxing in the bubbles so much more convenient – and you may have somewhere to rest your book, too.

◀ **Cross-head** style taps are the classic, timeless choice and a great way to give even the blandest white suite a traditional touch. These wall-mounted designs are a contemporary option for a more streamlined bathroom.

▼ **A** dark wood, freestanding towel rail is a wonderful accessory and true to Victorian style. Otherwise look out for simple bar-style rails in chrome or gold with ball finial ends to attach directly to the wall for a similarly period look.

COUNTRY STYLE 2

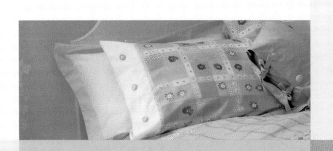

2 COUNTRY STYLE

Charming and homely, country style has a timeless appeal that can be adapted to almost any home. Informal mix-and-match furnishings and natural wood furniture are the essential starting point for both fresh modern country looks or rich and earthy traditional country style.

You don't have to live in a cottage to decorate in a country style. This soft, informal look is perfect for creating a relaxing yet cosy and welcoming mood in any house. The feel can be pure classic country or given a contemporary twist, depending on the colour schemes you choose and how you interpret the theme to suit your personal style. If you prefer a really rustic look, then opt for richer colours and mix with more heavily patterned fabrics such as chintzes and mid- to dark-toned woods. If you want a fresher, more modern feel, lighter shades combined with a more pared-back mix of patterns and textures will give you the essence of country style but without the flounces. Comfort is the golden rule for furniture and mixing old items with new is the easiest way to capture that lived-in, rustic feel. Avoid heavily dressed or ultra-sophisticated window treatments and go for simple cotton curtains with a pencil-pleat heading instead. Cosy clutter adds the essential finishing note and accessories such as photos and pictures are the ultimate way to stamp your character on your home.

◀ **Country style can be surprisingly modern if you cut back on the frills. This living room has been given a charming rustic feel with a mix of different upholstery fabrics, ranging from a plain denim-blue sofa to a blue and white chequered footstool, both of which are fairly minimal in style. However, the essential country elements are still apparent, from the large-motif floral roman blind to the wooden floor, a chunky pine coffee table and shelves full of personal possessions.**

◀ It is tempting to stick to antique pine furnishings in the dining room, but painted furniture that has been distressed around the edges for an aged look is equally charming. Pale paint finishes keep a light and airy feel where solid wood might look too dominant. Rush seats on the ladder-back chairs complete the relaxed mood.

key characteristics

- **Aged furniture in chunky designs** rather than neat and polished antique or period pieces. Do not worry if wooden furniture looks a little worn around the edges – distressed items are ideal for an authentic country look. Also keep an eye out for heavy twisted legs on gate-leg tables and on dressers.

- Lots of **rustic mid-toned woods**, such as pine and oak for floors, furniture and even walls.

- **Floral fabrics** are essential but need to be teamed with an eclectic mix of patterns for upholstery and curtains to avoid looking too neat and new.

- **Simple window treatments**, so no grand swags or tails.

- **Natural textures**, from wooden panelled walls to Aran-knitted cushions and throws, for a homespun atmosphere.

- **Displays of china**, personal possessions and photographs on walls, shelves and bookcases or dressers in every room.

▶ The colours of nature are often the inspiration behind a country look. Here the yellows of primroses have been used to create a look that is feminine and fresh. Gingham, large checked and striped fabrics combine to add subtle pattern; a beech laminate floor adds a modern note and the iron bedstead is authentic country.

is this **the right look** for me?

Country style is ideal for you if you:
- ✔ love **relaxed, informal** room designs
- ✔ prefer homes with **character** and a **sense of history**
- ✔ like to **mix old and new** for individual style
- ✔ want a **personal** rather than a fashionable look
- ✔ do not worry when guests call round and the house is **not immaculate**
- ✔ have a **large family** and/or **lots of pets**

Avoid if any of the following is true:
- ✘ I **hate clutter** and knick-knacks
- ✘ **Pared-back minimalist** room schemes suit my need for order
- ✘ I am **nervous of mixing** and matching different furniture and accessories
- ✘ I prefer **coordinated soft furnishings**, such as matching curtains, cushions and lampshades
- ✘ I like everything to look **fresh, new** and **up to date**

COLOUR

The country palette takes its inspiration from the world of nature, so it is always easy to find a starting point for a room scheme – just think of the colours of flowers, leaves and grasses. There are two basic palette options, depending on whether you want to create a fresh, modern look or favour a more rustic finish. You must choose one palette rather than mix and match the two, but both provide ample flexibility for an entire home. Consider lime-washed or pale oaks with the fresh palette and pine or antique oak for the earthy palette.

modern country

This is based on lighter, fresher colours and will suit less cluttered room layouts. Colours include the pretty pastel shades you might see in a cottage garden flowerbed, such as primrose yellow, cornflower blue, soft apple green and rose pink. Looking best in a room with light, rough-plastered walls, these colours suit simple fabrics such as two-tone checks and stripes, and painted woodwork. They also work well in rooms where size is an issue and natural daylight is scarce.

• Think **ice-cream colours**
TONES LIKE:
    primrose yellow
    soft apple green
    cornflower blue
    rose pink

TEAM WITH:
* **simple patterned fabrics (checks and stripes)**
* **painted woodwork**

colour tips

- **One colour to avoid** in any country colour scheme is brilliant white, which looks too stark and cold. Opt instead for off-white alternatives, including chalk, string, ivory and cream, for the softness you need.
- **Although country style** requires lots of layers of colour, from walls to carpets to upholstery, you still need to be careful not to overload each room. The balancing act is to achieve a naive, informal mood, not a mish-mash of clashing shades. Limit yourself to three or four colours per room used in various intensities; or choose just two colours and white for the most simple style. Finding a patterned curtain or sofa fabric you love is the easiest starting point as most patterns have at least three shades. Carry this swatch with you at all times as reference for your paint, wallpaper and carpet choices, then match each as closely as possible to one of the accent colours in the patterned fabric and you'll have the perfect blend of toning colours on walls, floors and furniture. Walls work best when all four are painted or papered in just one colour or design. Paint ceilings soft white.

traditional country

The classic country palette has a more earthy quality, with shades becoming richer and deeper – bluebell blue, sage green, rich brown-toned reds – to create a more rustic feel. A soft tonal quality is what you need, with no single colour dominating. Painted brick walls and stone flooring look wonderful with rich floral fabrics. Such colours suit cosy living rooms and dining rooms in particular and are best teamed with large-scale dark wood furniture.

- Think **rich earth colours**

TONES LIKE:

- mustard
- sage green
- bluebell blue
- rich brown-toned reds

TEAM WITH:

- **bare brick walls and stone flooring**
- **rich floral fabrics**

WALLS

No wall in a real country cottage is ever completely smooth or perfectly vertical, so it is worth thinking about adding textured finishes to your walls as an easy way of replicating that slightly raw, unfinished feel. It need not be a long-term commitment.

Of course, if your walls are already imperfect, so much the better! There are many ways to add a textured finish, from thick textured paints (the modern, more user-friendly versions of Artex, for example) to panelling and even blown vinyl wallpapers. The main consideration is to ensure that the option you choose is not difficult to remove at a later date should you tire of the scheme. Plain coloured walls are your best bet, allowing you to layer on patterns in the form of curtaining, soft furnishings and accessories.

But patterned wallpapers, such as blowsy rose motifs, echo the theme beautifully too and will not overwhelm if you cover just one focus wall.

Add hand-stamped motifs to walls with paint and a rubber stamp for a homespun feel; there is no need to measure out a perfectly regular pattern. Tongue-and-groove and wooden wall panelling with an obvious grain make a lovely connection with the natural world and are far easier to fit than you might imagine. Anyone with basic DIY skills could easily cover a wall in a day.

◄ **Floral wallpapers,** especially those in pastel tones, set a pretty and feminine scene and look wonderful in bedrooms. Small spriggy prints work well on all walls in the room, but large designs like blowsy roses will look fabulous in smaller doses – for example, to create an eye-catching focal wall behind a bed.

▶ **Stamped walls have all** the impact of wallpaper but with the added fun of creating the look freehand, using paint and a rubber stamp motif of your choice. Here two sizes of stamp and three paint colours have been used to transform a bedroom wall in just one hour.

▼ Rough-plaster effects mimic the look of irregular cottage walls and can be faked quite easily with the special paints now available. It is sensible to hang lining paper first so the texture is easy to remove when you fancy a change.

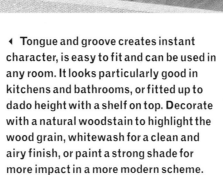

◄ Tongue and groove creates instant character, is easy to fit and can be used in any room. It looks particularly good in kitchens and bathrooms, or fitted up to dado height with a shelf on top. Decorate with a natural woodstain to highlight the wood grain, whitewash for a clean and airy finish, or paint a strong shade for more impact in a more modern scheme.

▲ Wood panelling adds a touch of rustic charm to a hallway and is relatively easy to fit with the DIY kits now available. This dado-height panelling adds character without overpowering a small space and would look equally lovely painted. Choose a design with skirting to match if you can.

FLOORS

Think practical rather than pretty when it comes to choosing cottage-inspired flooring and you will not go far wrong. As true country home owners know only too well, fluffy carpets do not stand a chance against muddy boots, soggy dogs and all the treasures cats and kids drag in.

Hard flooring is the most authentic choice for country-style floors and there are a huge variety of materials to choose from. The bumpy, natural textures of stone flooring, such as terracotta, slate and even sandstone, add an earthy, back-to-nature feel. They are also incredibly durable, making them perfect for rooms that connect directly with the great outdoors – your hall, kitchen or conservatory for example. Just bear in mind that they can be unforgiving to your feet and offer no protection in the kitchen where dropped crockery is

almost guaranteed to smash on impact. You can, of course, fake the finish with lookalike vinyls for a warmer, cushioned end result. Wooden flooring, in the form of either wood-effect laminate, pine floorboards or solid wood such as oak, echoes that same essential connection with the natural world, as do natural fibre carpets such as sisal and coir which are rough and rugged. No one is really going to argue if you use carpet in bedrooms and rooms where softness and cosy toes are a must.

▸ **Terracotta tiles are warmer underfoot than some stone floors and add a rich colour to rooms which ages well with time. They can be stained easily by water and other spillages, so most terracotta tiles need specialist sealing.**

▸▸ **Wood laminates give you the effect of wood on a tighter budget and are still very hard-wearing, although you cannot sand them back and revarnish as dents and flaws appear with time. Also, they are not really suitable for humid rooms, such as the family bathroom, where water can seep between the tongue-and-groove joins and cause warping.**

◄ Slate or quarry tiles come in a range of shades from blacky-grey through to copper tones with a beautifully irregular patina and a slightly bumpy texture, which makes them very pleasing to the eye. They age well and are resistant to staining but can be cold and hard underfoot.

◄ Sanded floorboards are a great cost-conscious option if you are lucky enough to have them. Hire a **DIY** floor-sander (not dissimilar in appearance to a vacuum cleaner, with sandpaper instead of carpet brushes) and a smaller hand-held orbital sander to reach right to your skirting. Sand to an even texture and protect with at least two coats of satin-finish purpose-made floor varnish for a durable end result.

▶ Natural floor-coverings like this rib-weave coir add a rustic touch for country-style floors. Coir is particularly hard-wearing and durable, although it is not suitable for humid rooms, such as the bathroom.

FABRICS

'Mix and match' is the key when choosing fabrics for country-style upholstery and soft furnishings. This means mixing textures and different-sized patterns for a look that appears to have been created over time instead of the perfectly coordinated style that is seen in show homes.

Forget borders that match curtains that match bedlinen, and have fun blending fabrics together. Ginghams, checks and florals are essential elements. The way to ensure that they sit happily together without overwhelming a scheme is to restrict yourself to a colour palette of three or four shades running throughout. Tiny gingham and tiny floral prints are ideal for more feminine schemes, and bigger square patterns and the odd impressive floral motif work well if you prefer a bolder, more modern feel. However, with bigger prints you need to be careful to avoid pattern overload. Do not be afraid to throw in a few stripy items for good measure in complementary shades. Crisp cottons and slubby linens are more in keeping with country style than chenilles and damasks. Remember that durability and stain resistance are essential for any fabric or finish in the hard-working country home so buy materials for upholstery and curtains that will withstand a machine wash rather than dry-clean only alternatives.

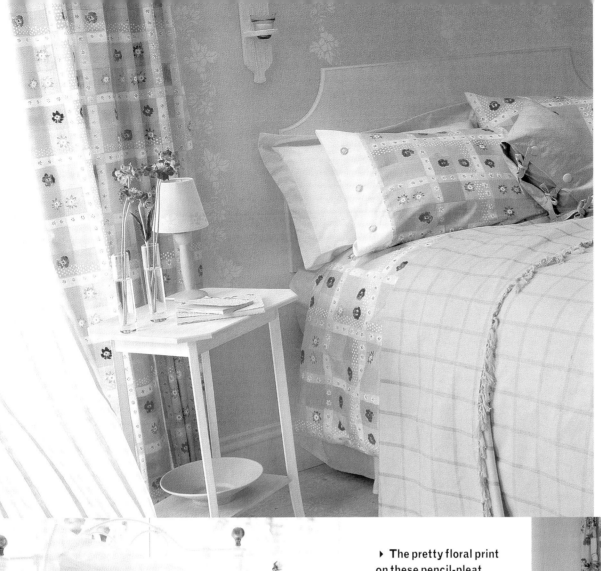

◁ Inspired by the colours of spring, this feminine bedlinen uses the whole range of the more modern country palette – primrose yellow, apple green, cornflower blue and rose pink. It provides plenty of flexibility for updating the scheme quickly by simply changing the wall and headboard to another of the toning shades.

▷ The pretty floral print on these pencil-pleat curtains adds just the right level of country style and teamed with white walls looks surprisingly smart. The curtains could be lined inside with a contrasting plain or tiny check fabric in a toning shade of blue for interest when pulled back. This also gives you the option of reversible curtains for a two-in-one look.

◁ Ginghams, stripes and even polka-dot fabrics mixed together give a country flavour for those who prefer to avoid floral motifs. But you could easily mix in a flowery cushion or two if you like, as plenty of pattern is integral to the informality of country style.

KITCHEN

The ultimate country kitchen combines fitted and freestanding units to create a look that feels as if it has evolved with time rather than been designed to order. Mixing old and new adds character and a sense of history. You are not aiming for anything too neat or perfect here.

Your choice of units will depend entirely on whether you want a traditional cottage feel or something with a more modern twist. Antique pine units and mid-toned oak are wonderful for classic country looks, while simple Shaker-style doors with their single-panelled design and wooden knobs create a fresher feel. With the latter, you have added flexibility in that you can choose from maple, beech and even painted finishes. Open-access storage is essential for that slightly cluttered, random look. Rattan baskets make wonderful holders for anything from linens to vegetables; open shelving lets you show off an eclectic selection of china, and a saucepan rack is another must to capture the informality of this style. Think carefully, too, about your choice of appliances. High-tech stainless steel will throw the theme off kilter. An enamelled Aga and a ceramic butler-style sink are perfect choices, but if budget and practicality won't allow then buy a soft cream oven and a Corian® sink to echo authentic style.

▲ **Tea towels make brilliant instant curtains in a country scheme. Hang them with curtain clips on a dowelling rod or stretch-to-fit curtain rod about halfway up your window for a touch of café style.**

kitchen essentials

✔ **freestanding** butcher's block
✔ **dresser** displaying china
✔ wicker or metal **freestanding vegetable rack**
✔ wall- or ceiling-hung **pan rack**
✔ **mix-and-match china** on open display
✔ **painted or mid-tone wooden** cupboard fronts in a simple panel style

▶ **Mix-and-match china evokes real rustic charm in a kitchen. Combine plain and patterned pieces in toning shades collected from junk shops and car boot sales.**

◄ Opt for kitchen units with simple panelled doors. The central work island complete with butler sink and period-style swan-neck tap adds focus to the whole room.

▾ Pretty gingham fabrics make perfect seat covers for kitchen chairs. Here a tea towel has been used for a cheap yet hard-wearing alternative.

◄ Enamelware is another country essential – chunky and durable. Look for spring-fresh shades like this buttermilk yellow or a soft cream.

LIVING ROOM

Forget the TV as a focus – in the country living room, seating takes the fireplace as its central point for a scheme that puts family, friends and conversation first. Put an upholstered footstool instead of a coffee table in the middle to encourage visitors to put their feet up and relax.

A real log fire or wood-burning stove is the ultimate choice, but it is easy to get a similar effect with excellent-quality 'fakes' in the form of gas or even electric cast-iron stoves. A pine fire mantel also works well, or you could add a timber frame to a more formal existing fire surround to give an immediate rustic touch. It is essential to opt for an informal partnership of mismatched seating rather than an overly coordinated traditional three-piece suite. Have fun mixing and matching a checked armchair with a plain sofa for example and gingham cushions with floral curtains for instant charm that does not look as if you have tried too hard. Just be sure to keep to a colour palette of three or four shades and use them throughout the upholstery options for a successful combination of unmatched pieces.

▾ **Wicker baskets filled with logs by the fire convey the essential back-to-nature feel of country style perfectly. They are also a great way to store newspapers, magazines and general clutter, as they can easily be tucked away in a corner or under a coffee table.**

living room **essentials**

✔ **open fire** or wood-burning stove (or equivalent)
✔ **low, loose-covered** squashy sofa and non-matching chairs
✔ **side tables** and sofa-end lamps
✔ **lots of accessories** on display, from family photos, botanical or farmyard prints and clocks to candlesticks, plus magazines and books close to hand
✔ **fabric-covered footstool**, preferably on turned legs, or wicker chest

Fresh cottage garden shades of cornflower blue, fuchsia pink and primrose yellow give this charming lounge/diner a vibrant yet pretty look. Mix and match patterned fabrics, including florals and stripes, add an informal eclectic feel in the form of curtains and cushions. The warm wood furniture adds a soft honey glow, whereas whitewashed furniture might look too stark in contrast to the rest of the colour scheme.

Chintzy floral upholstery gives this squashy sofa a look of faded glamour which fits the shabby chic image of country style to perfection. Large-blooms can be overpowering, but here, used against plain walls, the look is surprisingly fresh and subtle.

Floral and gingham double-sided cushions give you maximum flexibility to update your scheme simply by turning them over to show off the other side. The pretty spriggy fabric design shown here is a good way to add a country touch to a plain or checked sofa.

BEDROOM

Settling back into plump pillows for breakfast in bed has to be what a country bedroom is all about. The comforting, laid-back scheme is ideal for lazy mornings sleeping in, or inviting the kids in to share toast and play on the bed while you read the papers.

◂ **One quick way to give an ordinary divan a cottage look is to paint a fake headboard on the wall behind the bed with a pretty floral or leaf stencil finish. Mask off a rectangle the width of the bed and about 60cm (2ft) higher than the top of the mattress, pull the bed away from the wall and paint with standard emulsion in a shade to contrast with the wall. A selection of nature-inspired prints will complete your new focal point.**

Too much clutter is never a problem in a cosy country bedroom, so the only thing you need to worry about is crumbs between the sheets! A chunky pine bedstead is true to this décor, but if you prefer a more delicate look a wrought-iron bedstead, preferably in black, is a lovely alternative. And a comfy, even battered armchair in a corner makes this a room to read in at any time of day. Fitted storage is definitely out, so choose a random selection of freestanding furniture instead. Start with a chunky chest of drawers with a traditional rocker mirror on top to double as a vanity unit, then add a weighty wardrobe, preferably with three drawers at base level, for the most authentic feel. To finish, all you need to add are the essential pine or fabric-covered linen chest at the end of the bed and a pretty cotton rug.

bedroom essentials

- ✔ **wood or wrought-iron** bedstead
- ✔ **freestanding wardrobe**
- ✔ **mix of antique pine** and painted furniture
- ✔ **natural textured** carpet
- ✔ **wicker or pine** linen chest at the end of the bed
- ✔ **folding screen**
- ✔ **woollen overblankets**

▸ **Layering different-textured linens on a bed adds to the cosy atmosphere of the country bedroom. Here, plain and patterned pillowcases convey an informal feel, while yet more pattern is provided by a subtly checked duvet cover. The Aran-knit throw suggests a homemade finish even though it is actually shop-bought!**

Autumnal hues on walls and at windows give this scheme an earthy, rustic look. Textured seagrass flooring, plant pictures on the walls and chunky wicker storage baskets under the bed all emphasize the links with the natural world. Aged pine furniture would work with this colour scheme, but the darker cherry tones add richness and a note of modernity, while checked blankets hung from curtain clips make wonderful curtains for an individual note.

Add quirky charm and brighten a bland bedroom wall with homemade foliage pictures in simple wooden frames. Here a family tree, in the truest sense, has been created by writing the names of family members on hand-painted leaves for a personal end result.

Leaf motifs suit country style perfectly if you prefer a cosier, more subdued look rather than fresh florals. You could use a rubber stamp or wallpaper to decorate entire walls, but leaf-print borders are a more sophisticated alternative and are so quick to do. Use them around the top of your room next to the ceiling, at dado height or butted up to a picture rail – all three work equally well. You could also consider revamping a chest of drawers by pasting leaf cutouts on to the front, then protecting them with a clear-varnish topcoat.

BATHROOM

Rustic accessories, distressed or aged furniture and a slightly unfinished quality are what give a country bathroom its charm. The aim is to create an informal, cosy room, ideal for family use and practical for children's bathtimes too.

Period-style suites are a wonderful starting point, especially retro 1930s designs, including a chrome shower/mixer tap. Although you might think a roll-top bath is too glamorous, it actually fits this relaxed, freestanding layout well if you have the space. Tongue-and-groove panelling on walls and bath panels suits the look, as do small sections of hand-painted tiles if you prefer a more patterned look. Then add a café curtain, shutters or a patterned blind to soften the window rather than going for something too sleek. Freestanding storage units add to the relaxed atmosphere. Choose wicker, pine, whitewashed or painted finishes to suit your colour scheme. Remember it's the details that really make the difference in this room. Fabric laundry bags hung on the back of a door, a freestanding Victorian-style pine towel rail, a wicker shopping basket for storing loose toilet rolls and a peg rail for toiletry bags all create the perfect homely finishing touches.

▸ This fresh blue and white colour scheme is a pared-back version of country style in that it appears less colourful and cluttered than you might normally expect. However, the easy informality, the slightly whimsical floral motif which has been stamped on to the walls and the gingham appliqué squares on the blind all mark this as a country bathroom. The wooden panelling to half wall height adds a charming period flavour and can easily be copied by attaching wooden battens to the wall to form fake rectangular panel surrounds. Paint both the battens and the wall left between in the same shade, then simply add a wooden shelf to complete the look.

bathroom essentials

✔ freestanding storage units with rattan drawers or **fabric-fronted doors**
✔ **wicker baskets** for holding toiletries
✔ mismatched **bottles of bath salts** and bubble bath on display
✔ **fabric woven** bath mat
✔ freestanding **towel rail**, preferably in stained pine
✔ towels with **hand-embroidered floral or leaf** motifs

▸ This unit with its gingham curtain provides practical yet pretty freestanding storage. You could easily recreate a similar look on an old piece of furniture with a panelled door. Remove the panel of wood and replace with glass instead, adding lightly ruched fabric either stapled or tacked inside.

▲ A gingham blind makes a charming choice for a small recessed window that would look overwhelmed by large drapes of curtaining fabric and is very practical in a bathroom. The tab-top heading provides an interesting detail.

◀ A wooden duckboard-style bath mat is a striking alternative to the usual woven variety and suits more modern country looks.

▶ This lattice-weave cabinet has been whitewashed with a distressed paint effect to make it look aged. To copy the effect, lightly sand your piece of furniture then rub a candle over sharp corners and edges – including door panels and anywhere that would usually be subject to wear and tear over the years. Paint lightly with your chosen matt shade. The paint will not adhere to the waxed areas, resulting in an aged look achieved in just an hour or two.

LOFT STYLE 3

3 LOFT STYLE

Contemporary furniture and innovative use of industrial materials, such as brick, steel and glass, are the essential ingredients for loft-inspired décor. The look suits open-plan warehouse apartments but it can easily be adapted to more humble suburban homes with judicious thought given to layout and lighting.

The loft apartment is a comparatively modern style choice, brought about by urban regeneration programmes and the conversion of old brick-built warehouses, factories and schools into large, airy open-plan homes. As happens with any movement, owners subconsciously began to conform to the modern décor style seen in this chapter to create a distinctive 'loft look'. Mixing modern textures such as glass and stainless steel with existing or salvaged building materials such as reclaimed floorboards and bare brick walls is the starting point for loft interior design. So although not everyone can attain the truly open-plan layout, it is incredibly easy to translate the main style elements to almost any home. White-painted walls or bare bricks create the required blank canvas for a combination of cutting-edge contemporary furniture and one-off salvage finds — say, a roll-top bath or a Victorian radiator. Above all, remember that maximizing the sense of space and juxtaposing old and new are the keys to creating a successful loft style.

◄ Glossy glass, chrome and pale wood against a backdrop of raw brick walls combine the essential elements of loft style all in one kitchen. The black leather dining chairs add a distinctly designer note but are now available from many high street stores at prices to suit every pocket.

◄ Minimal furniture and a neutral colour palette give this bedroom an almost Zen-like quality. The low-level wooden bed, sanded floorboards and streamlined blinds are all authentic to loft style. The room is prevented from looking too austere by layering textured fabrics on top of each other.

▲ In open-plan spaces, furniture needs to be used to create zones for specific activities. Here, two armchairs divide the living and eating areas while the far back wall is painted grey as visual separation of the dining space ... a trick that would work in your average house.

key characteristics

- **Walls painted in white matt emulsion**, bare brick or, for the ultimate urban feel, polished concrete.

- **Reclaimed floorboards** sanded and sealed with a light clear varnish, or real wood softened with the odd boldly coloured or softly shag-piled flokati rug.

- **Glass bricks** used as room dividers, particularly to separate a kitchen or bathing area. Sometimes also used instead of a window.

- **State-of-the-art appliances**, from stainless steel range cookers to eye-catching plasma- or flat-screen TVs.

- **A mix of ultra-modern light wood furniture** with ethnic or antique items adds interest to what might otherwise seem an anonymous space.

- **Larger-than-life seating**, particularly armchairs to loll in and sofas to stretch out on. Real loft spaces need drama to avoid looking empty and bland.

- **Open storage**, from two-sided shelving units that can be used as room dividers to box-style shelves that appear to float on the wall.

- **Furniture on wheels** for flexibility to alter layouts.

is this **the right look** for me?

Loft style is ideal for you if you:
- ✔ love **cutting-edge** furniture design and streamlined appliances
- ✔ prefer a life **without clutter**
- ✔ like **open, light** and **airy** spaces
- ✔ like one- or two-room **open-plan living** and minimalist style
- ✔ live in a **modern** house or flat

Avoid if any of the following is true:
- ✘ I need my own space to **escape the family** sometimes
- ✘ I want a home with a **cosy** atmosphere
- ✘ My **kitchen** is the heart of my house
- ✘ I hate the idea of **minimalist** design
- ✘ I have **quirky individual** taste in décor

COLOUR

Since loft style prides itself on individualism, this is one of the hardest schemes for which to prescribe a definitive palette. Some loft owners favour bold blocks of colour in vivid but not quite primary shades, while more minimalist decorators prefer to use graphic black and white and moody shades for a more deliberately urban look, to complement the brick and wood fabric of the building itself. Choose your colour palette depending on how expressive or industrial you want your home to be – or mix the two for variety from room to room.

• Think **rich off-primaries** and **smoky tints**

TONES LIKE:

- **brilliant white**
- **pale slate grey**
- **steel blue**
- **smoke**
- **mink**
- **saffron**
- **burnt orange**
- **red wine**
- **cobalt blue**
- **dragonfly green**
- **aubergine**
- **indigo**

TEAM WITH:

- **wooden floorboards**
- **distressed leather furniture in chocolate and tan**
- **glass and silver accessories**
- **stainless steel appliances**

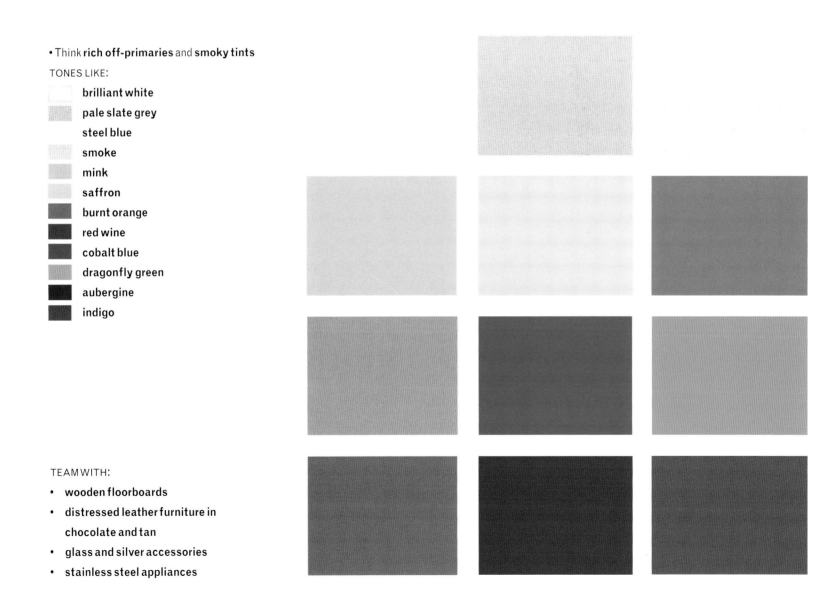

how to make it work

Bold colours bring focus to a large open-plan space but are best used sparingly, on no more than 25 per cent of the wall space in any one room. It is also wise to use just one bold shade per room. One **scarlet** or **indigo** wall, for instance, adds real drama to an all-white or brick scheme and can also be used to define a specific space. Painting the far end wall in a lounge/diner to highlight the dining zone and give it a different identity is a good example. Use the same shade in just a few accessories, such as a vase and a cushion, to create a subtle sense of continuity, always remembering that an obviously coordinated room scheme is entirely out of keeping with the basic beliefs of mix-and-match loft style. If bold, vivid colours are not your taste, you will love the smoky rich shades in the palette on the right, such as **moody aubergine** and **deep grey-green aqua**, which are softer on the eye and also a more sophisticated take on urban style. The other advantage of smokier shades is that you can use a wider variety of tones in one scheme to create a more harmonious and sophisticated overall feel.

CEILINGS

These should be **brilliant white** to maximize the sense of light and space in any room.

WOODWORK

Skirting boards and window frames should be in **natural wood** or painted in colours that melt into your overall scheme rather than being a feature in their own right. If you decide to go for wooden floors, sand back your skirting and finish with a clear satin varnish for protection or paint the same colour as the walls so they blend right in. Similarly, window frames are best painted in **white satinwood** or a matt finish, or left as natural wood.

WALLS

If you want to be truly authentic, bare brick walls or smoothed concrete finishes are the ultimate urban look and are found in every loft or warehouse conversion. So even if you live in a newly built apartment or home, it would be worth considering exploring whether at least one wall in your main living room could be returned to its original brick, or made to look like brick.

The other option is plain white emulsion on almost every wall to maximize light and a sense of spaciousness. Add your own personality with boldly painted focal-point walls, glass-brick dividing walls, stainless steel panels (like those used as splashbacks in the kitchen) and mosaic tiles for variety. You are aiming to combine raw industrial-inspired textures in small amounts with slick contemporary materials to create a very individual effect.

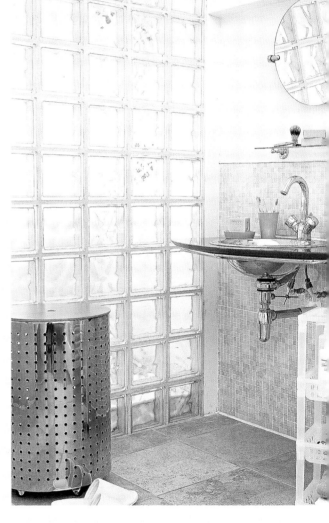

◄ White emulsioned walls emphasize the light and airy theme of this style of décor and act as the perfect blank canvas for bold, chunky furniture. Walls also benefit from the odd large-scale modernist painting.

▲ Glass bricks feature heavily in loft design and are often used to create entire walls to divide the open-plan space into specific areas. Here they have been built to form an eye-catching customized shower enclosure.

◂ **O**ne boldly painted focal wall is a good way of adding drama and interest to a minimalist loft scheme. **C**hoose colours such as cobalt blue, scarlet, fuchsia and deep terracotta, depending on your furnishings, for maximum impact – this is no place for a subtle voice.

◂ **M**osaic tiles are absolutely essential, whether for a kitchen splashback or used floor to ceiling in a bathroom. **C**hoose all one shade for a municipal swimming pool feel.

▸ **S**teel tiles or sheeting are a wonderful way to give walls a high-tech look in a loft kitchen – if you can bear the regular polishing necessary to maintain the look.

FLOORS

Using salvaged floorboards throughout a loft-style home captures the warehouse feel perfectly, as they were the material most commonly used in that type of building. They are also one of the most practical and durable choices to run through an entire interior.

If you are interpreting loft style in a modern home, real wood or laminate flooring fakes the same effect but is more accessible to purchase. Just remember to add the essential rug or two to soften the look and define different living zones. The bathroom is the only room in which flooring generally differs from the rest of a loft, for reasons of hygiene and practicality. Here mosaic tiles or enormous stone-look slabs offer the perfect waterproof alternative to wood for a slick city feel.

◀ **A cream flokati rug** adds softness to a wood laminate floor for a touch of retro 1970s appeal and is a treat for the toes after hard flooring throughout the rest of the interior.

▲ **Metal tread-plate tiles** add industrial chic to loft-inspired kitchens, with the added advantage of being incredibly durable and surprisingly hygienic. They blend beautifully with your stainless steel appliances for a slick, continuous theme.

◂ Real cowhide rugs are an increasingly popular choice to add a dramatic statement to loft flooring. Tan and white gives a richer look than black and white.

▸ Naked floorboards are the ultimate choice. Loft owners generally have the luxury of simply sanding back and varnishing original flooring but if you are recreating the look at home and starting from scratch, sourcing reclaimed flooring from local salvage yards will win you lots of style points. Also keep your eyes open for buildings in your local area that are being revamped or demolished and find out what the developers might be throwing away.

◂ Smooth stone or creamy ceramic tiles laid in large slabs add sophisticated city chic to bathrooms for a waterproof, easy-clean finish. Here, the high-gloss surface contrasts beautifully with matt mosaic wall tiles while creating a restful floor for an understated elegance.

FABRICS

Texture and colour rather than pattern are key when choosing materials to suit your loft-style home, so you should be mixing raw and rough with sleek and bold. A battered leather armchair teamed with a velvet-covered sofa is the perfect example.

Apart from leather, suede is a wonderful texture to introduce and is most commonly seen on cushions, cube-style footstools and even bed throws. Felt is something else that feels good and can be used for rugs and even roller blinds. Window treatments otherwise tend to be hard and streamlined, so look out for wooden slatted blinds, Perspex shutters or steel venetian blinds. Crisp white cotton roller blinds are also a good alternative, but consider the pull-up rather than roll-down variety for a more modern twist. Finally, although pattern is kept to a minimum, it is helpful for adding interest to excite the eye in an open-plan home, providing spots of visual focus to avoid a bland if minimal result. Always go for bold statement fabrics rather than prissy little prints, which are wholly out of keeping with this high-contrast décor. Using tartan is not unheard of and animal prints are particularly popular, especially zebra, leopardskin and cowhide, which make dramatic choices for floor rugs and cushions.

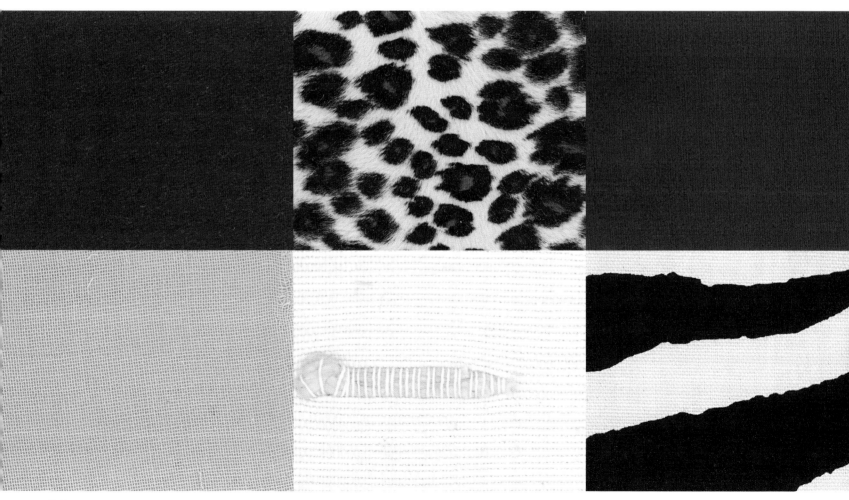

◀ **S**uede, soft jersey and white linen create layers of texture for interest in a loft bedroom. Try suede lookalikes, which are machine washable to keep life easy and stop you having to worry about spillages. The new fakes are incredibly realistic, even to the touch.

◀ **I**ndulge your secret exhibitionist side and go wild with a leopardskin print-upholstered armchair for instant impact. Just one item like this can totally transform your room and ensure a minimalist contemporary look is anything but bland.

▶ **A**lpaca, cashmere and bobbly textured upholstery are all unusual luxury fabrics which fit perfectly in any loft-inspired room. Show off the texture to best effect by choosing rich, deep shades such as chocolate, or pure cream if pet hairs and small sticky fingers are not an issue in your home.

KITCHEN

Despite the reality of urban life, with meals on the run and regular eating out, the loft kitchen takes inspiration from the glamorous semi-professional kitchens of the celebrity chefs seen on TV. Gleaming stainless steel appliances are teamed with tiled or wooden flooring and units in brushed-silver finishes, pale beech or Shaker styles.

Freestanding kitchen units keep this room true to the unfitted open-plan look. So, while one wall might feature fitted units for maximum storage, these will be combined with a butcher's block work-top on wheels, and always the ubiquitous six-ringed steel range cooker. Retro bulbous-shaped fridges in palest blue, aqua, cobalt, scarlet or even pastel pink are immensely popular too. Standard-sized ceramic tiles look completely out of keeping with the loft-look kitchen, so consider instead single-colour mosaic tiles for use in the space between your work-tops and wall-hung cupboards. A panel of stainless steel, cut to fit, makes a dramatic alternative as a splashback for sinks or your range cooker and is a very common feature ... but safety glass in a green-tinged finish with the wire grid visible is another great choice to echo the industrial inspiration. Finally, make provision for open access storage including wall-hung box shelves with hidden fixtures so that they appear to float on your walls. Catering style metal bar shelving works brilliantly too.

kitchen essentials

- ✔ **stainless steel oven** or range (choose brushed aluminium if you hate cleaning off fingerprints)
- ✔ one-colour **mosaic tiles** – especially cobalt blue, white or stone tones
- ✔ mobile **butcher's block**
- ✔ stainless steel or **glass splashback**
- ✔ **stainless steel** extractor hood
- ✔ mix of **freestanding** and fitted units
- ✔ wall-hung **open shelving** for easy access
- ✔ retro-style **freestanding fridge**
- ✔ pale wood, white gloss or **brushed metal-effect** cupboard doors in softly moulded or Shaker panel style
- ✔ **halogen spotlights** on wire tracking stretched across the ceiling

▼ **A stainless steel cooker is an absolute essential for the loft kitchen. If you have space for a range, go for a design with an integral extractor hood and stainless steel wall-panel splashback for maximum impact. Even if you do not cook much, it will look as though you do!**

▶ **Round sinks hung below work-top level create a modern, clean professional look. Tuck one into a corner of your kitchen for clever use of minimal work-top space.**

▾ One wall of units is the only concession here to the average kitchen. The high-tech central island is the focus of the room and is used as a visual divider between the kitchen and general living space. Glossy steel, wood, laminate, plastic and granite are all mixed to provide diversity of texture and a strikingly contemporary look, while open storage on glass shelves fixed to a fireman's-style pole emphasizes the open-plan feel.

▸ Metal venetian blinds give a crisp, streamlined look to windows, leaving the frame free and uncluttered. Curtains play no part in loft style, so if you must have softness simply add plain rectangular floor-length panels on the plainest of curtain poles at either side of windows with venetian blinds.

▾ Wall-hung racks for open-plan easy-access storage are popular and suit the semi-professional kitchen to perfection. Choose glass shelves on metal supports or these industrial-style steel rods. Factory outfitters make ideal hunting grounds for such racks.

LIVING ROOM

In true loft apartments the living room area is separated off from eating, cooking and sleeping zones only by the way furniture is arranged. But even if your room is enclosed you can still take inspiration from the contemporary shapes and materials.

You might not be able to squeeze in the authentically enormous four-seater sofa, but you can copy the look by teaming a more sensible-sized option in either cream or bold-hued upholstery, such as cobalt blue, terracotta or deep wine red, with a couch potato's dream of a leather armchair. All you need to add then is a minimalist wooden or glass coffee table, preferably on wheels – or, indeed, a Thakat Indian coffee table if you want to add a cross-cultural statement – and a large fluffy-textured flokati or bold geometric rug to soften your floorboards. In a real open-plan space the rug acts as a strong visual device to hold the living room space together. State-of-the-art home entertainment is proudly on display, with brand names an important consideration. The enormous flat-screen TV and the music system are style statements just as much as the furniture.

▼ **This boldly coloured futon-style daybed adds a quirky contemporary note to a loft scheme. The vibrant cobalt-blue upholstery makes a dramatic contrast against stark white walls and is one of the preferred accent colours for the loft look.**

living room **essentials**

- ✔ **mobile** coffee table or shelving unit
- ✔ **leather armchair** – either designer (Balzac being the ultimate label) or battered 'antique'
- ✔ **large rug**, preferably in a bold colour
- ✔ suede, felt and **leather cushions**
- ✔ **suede cube** for use as a footstool or additional seat
- ✔ **outsized sofa** in bold upholstery
- ✔ **eye-catching TV**

The masculine black leather furniture shown has a distinctive cube shape to add a sharp city feel to this living space. Enormous windows are left undressed to allow in maximum light while plain brick walls emphasize the urban setting. Furniture has been carefully laid out to create specific zones for living and eating with two armchairs acting as a visual break with their backs to the dining space. A large floor rug further defines the sitting area.

An open-sided shelving unit provides a clever way to divide an open-plan space without blocking out valuable light.

A fuchsia-pink plastic side table adds a funky futuristic look, emphasizing the use of old and modern materials in one room scheme.

BEDROOM

The formula for a loft bedroom is less easy to identify as it depends entirely on whether or not the room is divided from the rest of the apartment. This gives those with average-sized homes more ideas to experiment with when recreating loft style.

Many real-life loft apartments have the bedroom on an open-plan galley above the main living space, the result being rather impersonal, with room for just a bed and a bedside table or two. But a dividing wall will make a more personal haven. Low-level beds with the mattress centred in the middle of a wood surround on a slatted base are one of the most common choices, echoing minimalist or oriental influences. Ultra-modern metal bedsteads in chrome or brushed-silver finishes are another chic alternative. Normally the room has little other furniture except for streamlined storage to hide away clutter, or a shop-style hanging rail that can be moved around the room. Cupboards might be wall to wall and floor to ceiling in pale wood or glossy laminate. Frosted glass doors look very sophisticated but are only for the tidiest of owners.

▼ **House plants as accessories need to be structural and dramatic rather than floral and twee. These succulents in aluminium pots add just the right note to an empty windowsill.**

bedroom **essentials**

✔ **minimalist bed** in pale wood or silver-finish metal

✔ sleek, almost **invisible storage**, generally in the form of wall-to-wall cupboards

✔ **enormous mirror**, which sits on the floor against one wall to reflect maximum light and emphasize the feeling of space

✔ varnished floorboards or **real wood** flooring

✔ **white bedlinen** or with minimal pattern

✔ **wall reading light**s fitted above the bedhead

▶ **Lack of clutter is essential in any loft room but especially the bedroom and bathroom. Floor-to-ceiling cupboards are a wonderful solution for hiding away personal possessions and this frosted-glass, silver and white laminate option is a high-tech choice if you want to take loft style to its extremes.**

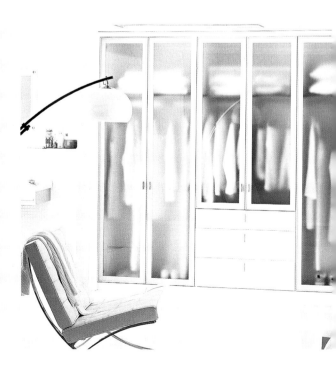

◀ **Neatly symmetrical cubes built to cover an entire wall can house anything from designer accessories to books. They could even hold clothing if it was stored in metallic containers to ensure a clean, uncluttered finish.**

▼ **Mixing modern and traditional influences is part of the fun of loft-style décor. Here the owner has created a twist on the traditional four-poster bed, opting for an all-metal structure in modernist silver using industrial scaffolding to create the frame. Setting the bed centrally means that the rest of the room is left completely clutter free, emphasizing once more the feeling of light and space.**

BATHROOM

Sleek, almost clinical lines characterize the urban bathroom and a freestanding bath is the ultimate accessory, be it a roll-top with period taps to hint at the loft's history or a chic designer double-ender with wrap-around ergonomic panel and a floor-standing tap.

Of all the rooms in the loft apartment, this is the one where contemporary style is often taken to extremes. The ubiquitous mosaic tiles cover walls and floor for a municipal swimming pool look, while steel, glass – frosted and clear – and matt ceramics make up the other surfaces. Only the odd fluffy towel breaks the smooth-textured look. Recessed ceiling spotlights cast clear bright light over the room – and will show up every fingerprint and water mark unless you are extremely vigilant. A walk-in shower, preferably with a period-style large chrome rose shower head fitted into the ceiling or high on the wall, adds maximum impact. This awesomely beautiful style of room is suitable only for the tidiest of couples or singles, as the tiled surfaces are not family-friendly or as safe as they need to be for children.

▸ High-tech glass and neutral colour schemes are the first choice, but bold primary shades fit the loft look equally well, as this scheme proves. Here, in a modern twist, the freestanding bath is mixed with a neat wall-hung suite, cobalt-blue wall and lime-green mosaic tiles for an energizing end result.

bathroom **essentials**

- ✔ **walk-in shower cubicle**, preferably either a quadrant all-glass design or a purpose-made enclosure built from glass bricks
- ✔ **freestanding bath**, either a roll-top or a designer double-ended bath
- ✔ **unusual basin**, either retro 1930s design or ultra-modern glass or stainless steel wall-hung basin with the metal U-bend polished and on show
- ✔ one-colour **mosaic tiles** fitted floor to ceiling on at least one wall and preferably the floor, too
- ✔ **wooden decking** bath mat
- ✔ stainless steel or **matt white** ceramic accessories
- ✔ **open glass** shelves
- ✔ **chrome** heated towel rail
- ✔ recessed **halogen spotlights**

◂ Texture and interest are created here with a wood-slatted venetian blind that covers most of one wall and dramatic use of downlighters either side of a mirror to create focus at the far end of the room.

▸ **A slick wall-hung basin** is another essential to help create the illusion of yet more space. This glass and steel surround transforms an otherwise unremarkable white ceramic sink into something that is really eye-catching.

▴ **This gorgeous steel-finished double-ended** freestanding bath is pure designer style and is perfect for the loft look if you have the cash to splash. If money is tight, use it as inspiration and clad your old bath panel in brushed aluminium or galvanized steel to mimic the urban look.

ORIENTAL STYLE 4

4 ORIENTAL STYLE

Calm and tranquil, oriental style is the perfect grown-up choice for those who need their homes to be a relaxing haven after a hectic day. It is a look that cannot be achieved by half measures, but with such focused design rules to follow it is also one of the easiest themes to pull together.

Modern interpretations of oriental style

(on which this chapter concentrates) border on minimalism, although, as you can see from the colour palette and choice of fabrics, it is easy to add softness with 'floriental' motifs and hints of pastel shades. These serene, pared-backed room schemes are best suited to disciplined home owners who have the patience and willpower to keep rooms clutter free to ensure the look works to maximum effect. They are best avoided by families except those with the tidiest of children. The upside is that oriental décor is very distinctive, with strong guidelines as to furniture, colour palette, floors and walls, so, like a recipe, it is one of the easiest looks to follow for a successful end result. It also translates to almost any type of home, from loft apartment to town terrace – the thatched cottage being a possible exception. Look out for simple, low-level furniture in either the darkest of woods (wenge, black ash and mahogany) or palest birch, beech and even white gloss laminates. Cherry is also commonly used in the richer, more traditional Chinese-inspired schemes. Thankfully, because the look is uncluttered, you need only a few key pieces and accessories for each room, so it is fairly inexpensive to recreate at home.

▶ **A straight-hung fabric panel is an ideal streamlined treatment for the window. Here, delicate lotus-flower imagery adds prettiness to a very minimally furnished living room.**

▲ ▲ This streamlined and subtle room scheme features the white, silver and sage-green shades of the modern oriental palette and the characteristic low-level bed.

▲ This contemporary beech dining table has been styled to suit an oriental scheme by being teamed with black leather dining chairs, modern tableware, and an Eastern-inspired table decoration of bamboo stems. Authentic oriental dining features low-level tables with large floor cushions around them, but by using dramatic contrasts of tone in the room, the overall effect is very much the same while being practical for today's homes.

key characteristics

- **Low-level furniture, such as futon beds and seating, and floor cushions, to mirror Japanese and Chinese preferences for seating and sleeping close to the floor. It is essential that each piece is as simple and unfussy in design as possible. Sofas, for example, tend to be cube shaped and have tight backs rather than loose scatter cushions for the most streamlined effect.**

- **Dark woods like wenge or black ash are ideal for making the necessary dramatic contrast with light walls and floors, although bamboo or red-tinted rosewood is also authentic if you prefer a softer end result.**

- **Curtains are generally avoided as being too heavy and fussy. Go for minimalist treatments such as cream roman blinds or wooden venetian blinds instead.**

- **Accessories are kept to a minimum throughout in both modern and traditional oriental looks but may include delicate prints and wall hangings that feature birds, lotus blossoms or bamboo leaves, for example. Paper lanterns and lamps on the floor help create a soft glow at night-time without dominating the simple décor.**

- **Plain rather than pattern is the general rule for the modern oriental look, but if you want to add interest with pattern, chinoiserie is an oriental-inspired style of decoration, which uses quite lavish motifs – birds, dragonflies, pagodas and temples – for a more ornate finish with highlights of gold.**

is this **the right look** for me?

Oriental style is ideal for you if you:
- ✔ **hate clutter**
- ✔ want a strongly **identifiable theme**
- ✔ love **light and airy** room schemes
- ✔ like the idea of **minimalism** but could not be that extreme
- ✔ think the saying **'less is more'** is true for décor

Avoid if any of the following is true:
- ✘ I like furniture with **cosy cushions** you can really sink into
- ✘ I need a **kid-proof** home
- ✘ I like the flexibility to **change/update my look** regularly
- ✘ I have **lots of furniture** I'm not prepared to revamp or give up to create such a **regimented look**

COLOUR

Far Eastern-inspired décor falls neatly into two basic colour ranges. Traditional schemes have a flamboyant, opulent flavour with a regal palette of bold, contrasting shades suited to period homes. Modern oriental looks feature white walls, neutrals, bamboo green and even soft pastels for an altogether more pared-back look.

traditional oriental style

Rich and opulent, traditional Chinese looks use vivid shades such as lacquer red and navy, or prettier combinations of duck-egg blue, jade and lotus pink, teamed with many highlights of gold to create sumptuous, some might say ostentatious, effects. It is ideal for creating quite formal décor for older properties. Traditional Japanese style is far easier to emulate, focusing on a very minimal palette of black and white with accents of pure crimson red, but some may find this uncompromising to live with throughout a home.

• Think **richness** and **dramatic contrast**

TONES LIKE:

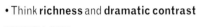 cream

 ginger

lustrous gold

jade

**Chinese
lacquer red**

navy blue

black

TEAM WITH:

- **gold accessories**
- **embroidered silk rugs and wall hangings**
- **ornately hand-painted ceramics such as lamps with ginger jar-style bases**
- **carpeted floors**
- **cherry, mahogany or lacquered furniture**

colour tips

The two basic colour palettes place a completely different emphasis on texture, with **traditional schemes** using high-gloss finishes on woodwork and furniture as an echo to its lacquered furniture. Even walls can be given a silken sheen, and this light-reflective effect is a good way to prevent the intense colours taking over a room. **Modern schemes**, however, work best with matt-finish paints and low-sheen textures, with woodwork finished in satin paint.

modern oriental style

Pared-back and simple, the modern oriental palette comprises the range of colours you will see in the majority of the room schemes shown on these pages. They are the easiest to copy successfully and the most soothing to live with. White or off-white walls are the standard background as dramatic contrast to dark wood furniture. Palest blossom pink and soft bamboo green are ideal for adding pretty femininity. The easiest modern palette of all is a mix of creams and bamboo beige with accents of silvery grey and sage green.

• Think **pale lotus flowers** and **nature-inspired hues**

TONES LIKE:

water-lily white	cherry-blossom pink
rice paper	orchid mauve
rattan beige	Japanese cherry
bamboo beige	
bamboo green	slate black

TEAM WITH:

- silver accessories
- wood, laminate or stone flooring
- ultra-pale or dramatically dark streamlined furniture
- paper screens and lighting

WALLS

If you opt for the modern oriental style, walls are incredibly easy and cheap to decorate as simple plain white or off-white emulsion is the most common choice throughout the house. Traditional style gives more room to experiment with pattern, gilding and bold shades.

Modern oriental décor demands unfussy walls as a backdrop to your streamlined selection of furniture, so you are not aiming for any great eye-catching effects. If that sounds too bland and boring, remember that dark wood furniture set against white looks incredibly dramatic, as does the odd carefully chosen print or wall-hung accessory, and you can also opt for pastel walls for versatility. However, if pattern and variety are essential to you, consider instead traditional oriental looks, which make opulent walls an integral part of any scheme, including gold-highlighted wall-coverings and bold paint shades such as lacquer red. The Chinese tend not to use much wall ornamentation, keeping pictures to a minimum and even then opting for delicate prints of lotus blossoms, birds and scenes taken from ancient Chinese lifestyles. Simple panels of calligraphy are another common choice. Take a trip to your local Chinatown for visual examples of patterns and colours used in real-life settings. It is a great excuse for a meal out!

◀ Matt and silk-sheen emulsion are both suitable, but in a fairly limited colour range – notably white and sage green. Traditional schemes tend to favour wallpaper, but for modern oriental looks painted walls are best, in pure white or, if you need a note of colour, lotus-blossom pink and seagrass green, as shown here.

▶ Oriental calligraphy makes a striking motif when painted as an eye-level border on a wall with a stencil. Just be careful to research the words or letters carefully so as not to offend.

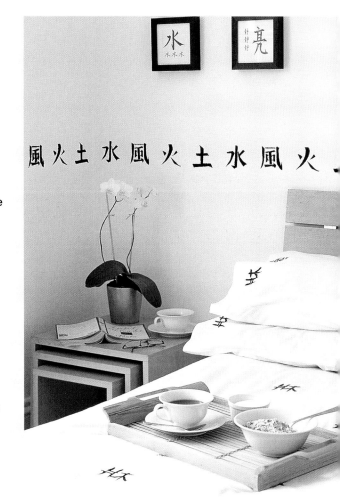

◀ **C**hinoiserie wallpaper featuring birds, temples, dragons and simple bamboo, sometimes with highlights of gold, is a pretty way to add focus, pattern and softness to a traditional oriental room scheme. **C**hoose pale colours and this look can be surprisingly subtle, or try a bolder look on just one focus wall for dramatic impact and contrast.

▶ **O**rnate fabric banners against plain white walls create a strong oriental statement in any room and look particularly striking hung above a bed or on a large living room wall. **T**hese can be made from chinoiserie fabrics, where motifs are similar to those shown on the wallpaper on the left.

▶ **A** pretty kimono hung on a wall can add an eye-catching and authentic detail to echo your oriental theme without spoiling the uncluttered look of the room.

FLOORS

Simplicity is key when choosing flooring for this look. As with the walls, the floor should be an unobtrusive base for the rest of your furnishings. Smooth textures with a slight sheen, such as laminate, marble or stone, all help add to the airy, spacious feel and are also easy to keep clean.

Carpet is almost never seen in the authentic oriental home, but you can cheat if you prefer this softer, warmer flooring underfoot by using ribbed or natural textured carpeting in neutral shades of cream, taupe and sand. Anything that echoes the natural world will not upset your scheme. Remember, though, to limit yourself to just two or three flooring options throughout your home. In this way you will keep to the streamlined look and avoid the visual jarring that arises with changes from room to room.

◄ **Bamboo laminate is the ultimate choice for perfectionists who want to ensure that their flooring is completely authentic. It has the added bonus of being hard-wearing and humidity-resistant, making it one of the wooden floors that copes best with kitchen conditions. As bamboo grows quickly, it is also a very environmentally friendly product.**

▲ **Woven or ribbed textured carpets in neutral tones fake the natural flooring look but will not stretch and they cope better with humidity, making them a safer option for those who prefer to stick to what they know best. They are suitable for every room.**

◄ **R**ush matting and canvas or woven rugs add instant echoes of oriental style, making them ideal for this look whatever your budget. **L**ook for sail cloth-weight canvas, leaving it plain for the cheapest option. **E**dge a natural carpet remnant with webbing tape or buy the ready-made alternative for ease and lay it on a wood-look or wooden floor.

▶ **B**lack slate provides dramatic contrast to minimally decorated walls and is a wonderful choice for both kitchens and bathrooms, and even hallways, being durable and relatively easy to keep clean if sealed well. **H**ere a silvery black manmade flooring fakes the same effect.

◄ **I**f you need to keep to a tight budget, floorboards sanded smooth and painted with clear varnish are the fastest, cheapest way to achieve your oriental style and they look wonderful. **T**hey can be a problem in bathrooms, because of water splashes, but even this can be overcome if you seal the gaps and apply at least three layers of heavy-duty yacht varnish to make them water resistant.

oriental style 89

FABRICS

Just because the oriental look is minimal, it doesn't mean you can't add texture and pattern with fabric. In fact, both are positively essential to avoid blandness. Imagery inspired by nature, such as birds and bamboo, is most common and can look incredibly subtle and delicate.

Natural-toned fabrics are the obvious and most foolproof choice, so slubby linens, brushed cottons, felt and bobbly alpacas are all worth considering, in tones of taupe, silver grey, ivory, cream, white and sand. Go for ribbed textures to echo the look of bamboo and do not be afraid of mixing in the odd minimally adorned fabric, such as a button-covered cushion. If the buttons are the same shade as the cushion itself, they will add visual interest without drawing your attention directly. Patterned fabrics are generally split into two

categories and your choice will depend very much on whether you are aiming for a modern oriental look or a bolder more traditional finish. For modern rooms, bamboo or delicate foliage-inspired motifs, scattered few and far between across a plain background is the look to shop for. Use on the odd scatter cushion or table runner as less is definitely more. Traditional settings can take more punchy, busy patterns such as twisting cherry blossoms, birds, pagodas and even pen-and-ink sketch-effect designs.

▼ Chinese calligraphy motifs add drama to any room. It would be overpowering if used in large sections but is the ideal accent choice for a curtain border, fabric wall panel or cushion cover.

◄ Inspired by courtesan clothing from the oriental courts, the delicately ornate patterning on this bedlinen shows that the oriental style can take on a prettier, more patterned feel if you choose to follow more traditional inspirations. Rich navy or cherry-red walls would make a striking backdrop and burnished gold accessories would look completely in keeping.

▲ A simple selection of linens in greys, taupes and whites, neatly folded across the bed, adds an Eastern touch. Apart from a sheer fabric panel, mirror and table with two pots, the room is kept almost completely accessory free.

KITCHEN

Cooking and entertaining are convivial yet simple matters in the modern oriental kitchen, where, as in every other room, the emphasis is on creating a minimal, uncluttered space using lots of pale colours and natural textures.

Oriental cooking tends to be fast and furious, so the space needs to be well planned, with utensils close to hand, lots of work-top space, a wok-friendly hob and a sensible layout to avoid accidents when moving quickly from fridge to work-top to oven. Oriental dining areas, when truly authentic, use seating at floor level to bring guests together in an incredibly intimate and yet simultaneously informal gathering. Of course, this is only suitable if none of your guests suffers from a bad back or creaky joints, and is totally impractical for a kitchen/diner. However, normal-height dining can easily be given an oriental twist through your choice of furniture, tableware and accessories for an elegant pared-back look. Chopsticks are optional!

kitchen essentials

✔ **natural wood, bamboo** or bold black or white glossy laminated units

✔ **granite, slate** or strongly coloured contrasting work-tops

✔ **white or black** square-shaped china

✔ **rush table mats** or bamboo roller table runner on a kitchen dining table

✔ **simple-shaped chairs** – for example, square, upright, plain-upholstered back and wooden legs – for a more modern scheme

✔ **wok**

◄ **A wooden dresser stained red makes a dramatic addition to a kitchen/diner and, with round black plates, has a particularly Japanese feel. You could create a similar look by staining unfinished solid pine with a mahogany or cherry woodstain or a more obvious red dye.**

▲ **Handleless cups are authentic for a Chinese tea ceremony and these with a bamboo-handled teapot will make a wonderful display on open shelving. Visit your local Chinatown for budget buys.**

There is no one typical style for oriental kitchen units but they should incorporate lots of fuss-free storage and provide easy access to utensils. As a guide, dark wood or white laminates tend to work best, with lots of contrast added via accessories – dark china, slate work-tops, white tiles and so on. With its bamboo detailing, this kitchen is by no means authentic, but few could doubt the theme intended.

Slate floor tiles make wonderful alternative table mats to suit this theme. Simply back the tiles with felt to avoid damage to your tabletops.

A white venetian blind adds textural interest and makes the perfect stream-lined window treatment, although bamboo and rattan look great too.

oriental style 93

LIVING ROOM

Streamlined style is as important as comfort in the oriental living room, with cube-shaped, preferably low-level furniture, and cushions kept to a minimum to avoid clutter. Think about the philosophy of yin and yang to create a high contrast colour scheme of dark and light.

All-white walls teamed with dark wood furniture are the epitome of modern oriental style, but if you have a family, introducing soft colours such as silvery grey, sage green and even lotus pink will make for a harmonious and more child-friendly feel. It is hard to get away from the sticky-finger factor, however, so do think carefully about your lifestyle before you opt for this look. Paper-shaded lights will help the scheme seem less minimalist and a paper, folding screen is a brilliant solution for hiding kids' toys in a corner to fake the requisite clutter-free finish without the hard work involved in continually tidying away. Keep accessories to an absolute minimum for display. Sleek ceramics in matt black or white are ideal, especially when in a symmetrical format, for example by placing a black wooden candlestick either side of a mantelpiece to echo the orderly formal rules.

▲ **Use bamboo laminate flooring to add a strong wood grain for interest underfoot. It is wholly in keeping with the Eastern theme.**

living room **essentials**

- ✔ **very dark** or very light wood furniture in streamlined designs
- ✔ **boxy simple-shaped** sofa with minimal cushions
- ✔ **low-level** wooden or rattan coffee table
- ✔ **floor cushions**
- ✔ **paper-lantern** lighting
- ✔ **rattan roller**, cream roman blind or tab-top curtain panels

▸ **In more minimalist room schemes, mixing textures is essential to avoid a bland end result. This soft cushion decorated with pearlized buttons adds visual interest and 'touch' appeal to a plain upholstered sofa, while just one black fabric cushion is all that is needed to add a dramatic touch.**

◂ **D**ark wood furniture provides essential contrast in the neutral living room, as this wenge console table shows. Just a few eye-catching pieces are all you need to add focal points around the room without overpowering and detracting from the simple décor.

▾ This tranquil, predominantly all-white living room features the key elements of modern oriental style. With its cube-shaped arms and simple white cover, the low-level sofa is suitably minimalist, softened only by a few scatter cushions. Billowing muslin curtains with a pretty hand-painted motif inspired by cherry blossom add a note of femininity.

BEDROOM

Primarily for sleeping rather than daytime relaxation, the oriental bedroom is a very restrained, simple affair. Its pared-back look is designed to remove distraction as you prepare for bed rather than create a cosy feel, so furniture is minimal and practical above all.

A futon bed is the key focus, although for the sake of comfort many people decide to use a low-level bed, preferably without a headboard, to create a similar look. Dress simply with plain white linens in cotton or jersey. Window treatments are simple and streamlined – roman blinds or wooden venetian blinds in preference to swathes of curtaining. Streamlined storage is essential to keep clutter out of sight, with floor-to-ceiling fitted wardrobes the favoured and most authentic option, although you can get away with freestanding furniture in natural textures, such as wicker and rattan, or items that have been designed specifically for an oriental theme. Accessories should also be kept to a tasteful minimum. A kimono wall hanging, a few bamboo stems in a vase, a picture and a mirror will usually be enough to complete your room.

bedroom essentials

✔ **low-level** or **futon-style bed**, preferably without a headboard
✔ **simple cube-shaped** bedside tables
✔ **pared-back window** treatments such as roman blinds
✔ **paper dressing screen**
✔ **rush mats** or natural seagrass carpet
✔ plenty of **unobtrusive storage** to hide clutter

◄ **Rattan furnishings add just the right amount of texture to a scheme to stop it looking bland. This neat six-drawer unit is ideal almost anywhere, be it in a bedroom, kitchen or hallway.**

▶ **A**n upholstered chair would be out of place in a minimally styled oriental bedroom, whereas this round wicker chair suits the look perfectly. **N**atural-toned cushions are all that is needed to add softness, and the fabric panel shown has a charming foliage motif which, although not authentically **C**hinese, fits seamlessly.

▲ Take inspiration from the Terracotta Army in China and create your own oriental focal points with figurines – from smiling Buddhas to these imposing warriors – on a mantelpiece or bedroom chest of drawers.

▲ Neutral shades from sand to caramel create subtle layers of colour in this tranquil bedroom, with a couple of dramatic black highlights in the form of trimmings and an oriental sculpture for a sophisticated yet subtle look. A rattan side table and ribbed carpet add textural interest to excite the eye and the thoughtful details even extend to the elegant oriental orchid in a pebble-decorated glass container.

▸ Chinese terracotta has a high-gloss glazed finish. Look out for pots and vases with a gold embossed image for the most authentic feel.

BATHROOM

Bathing as a means of relaxation is enormously important for oriental peoples and so, for them, the bathroom has become a sanctuary for ritualistic cleansing. If you love the idea of a serene scheme, this is the best bathroom style for you, providing you can keep it clutter free.

A sunken bath is the ultimate accessory, but if, as for the average home owner, this is simply too costly or difficult to fit in your home, you can create similar effects with a low-level bath that has stepped access. Luxurious, silky textures play an important role in creating a relaxing space, so consider smooth limestone or ceramic tiles underfoot (kept warm with underfloor heating for comfort), although smooth wooden decking can also work for a more modern effect – from a bath mat to an entire floor. Back-to-wall and wall-hung suites fit particularly well into an oriental scheme as they are designed to be installed so that none of the pipework is on display – perfect for a truly streamlined effect. Fitted bathroom cupboards in dark woods are a sensible addition to help you maintain a clutter-free end result by hiding loo rolls and everyday paraphernalia from view. Slatted wooden shutters, perspex panel shutters and bamboo or cream roller blinds are all ideal at windows. Then all you need add is candles for the perfect meditation zone.

▲ **Bamboo accessories fit the theme perfectly and add a layer of warmth and character to an otherwise minimalist scheme. Here woven-rush linen baskets and a seagrass room divider are used to create contrasting texture for visual interest and softness against stark white walls.**

bathroom **essentials**

✔ **limestone flooring**
✔ **slatted wooden** bath mat
✔ **sunken bath** or short but deep bath for seated bathing
✔ **all-natural** soothing colour scheme
✔ **slatted wooden** blinds

◄ **Dramatic black wenge wooden units with lattice front doors add a distinctive Japanese feel to this bathroom and provide ample storage to hide unwanted clutter.**

◄ **This** sleek, simple basin is made from recycled manmade materials for a seamless finish that apes the look of granite. Minimalist yet luxurious, it would add the perfect oriental twist to an otherwise standard white suite.

▾ Minimal detailing and a very simple, natural-themed colour scheme are the starting points for this oriental-style bathroom. The sunken bath is the luxurious choice, but a similar effect could easily be achieved by adding steps or sinking a double-ended bath into a wooden platform. Wooden flooring is not often advisable for a bathroom as it does not cope well with splashes. You can be a little more flexible in adults-only rooms, but it is also easy to fake the look with realistic wood-effect vinyls for a sleek, high-sheen floor.

▾ A woven blind in a rich natural tone adds warmth to a window yet retains the required streamlined finish. For bathrooms it is essential to choose blinds that have been treated to withstand humidity so as to avoid problems with mould and condensation.

FRENCH CHIC

5

FRENCH CHIC

Elegant and romantic, ornate but never ostentatious, French chic is a delicately sumptuous look perfect for those who yearn for a touch of luxury. It combines the muted colours of the Art Nouveau movement with ornate furniture reminiscent of 18th-century France and works best in moderately spacious, well-lit homes.

▶ **A sumptuously upholstered bed and gorgeously ornate pink marble fireplace create two dramatic focal points in this sensuous boudoir-style room. Soft tones of lilac and icy silver seal the feminine note, while a crystal chandelier adds the perfect finishing touch for an opulent period feel.**

As with chic French clothing, the key to success with this look comes down to buying a few eye-catching pieces and setting them against subtle colour schemes to create a look that whispers expensive even when it has been put together on a budget. The style suits townhouses and apartments with high-ceilinged rooms, and works to maximum effect in homes that are naturally light and airy, so as to make the most of the muted Parisian colour scheme. Rich textured velvets, silks and chenilles add opulence to soft furnishings, while silver leaf, crystal and beaded accessories bring elegance and sparkle to each room. French chic is certainly one of the more difficult looks to achieve, because the natural tendency is to over-accessorize. Less is definitely more to show the muted colour palette to best effect, so choose limited but ultra-elegant items. This is always going to be a high-maintenance look, but the returns will be well worth the effort.

key characteristics

- Scrolled metal furniture in delicate designs from dining and occasional chairs to hall tables and wrought-iron bedsteads. Look out for silver, soft gold or bronze rather than heavier-looking wrought iron.

- Sumptuous fabrics such as velvet, chenille, silk and linen in subdued shades, either plain or with delicate self-patterns, for a rich yet understated effect.

- Pelmeted or swagged window treatments plus shimmering voiles or organza sheers.

- Smooth textures, from sleek laminate flooring to velvet cushions and cool marble work-tops in a kitchen.

- Careful choice of accessories – less is definitely more in the French look, but what you do display should look top quality even if it is a junk shop find.

- Mirrors and crystal to reflect maximum light, and candlelight to enhance the sense of luxury.

▲ This Louis XVI sofa is the ultimate choice for a French chic living room scheme, but unless you stumble across one in a junk shop, they can be rather expensive. It might not be ideal for lolling around on, but is perfect for adding an authentic touch of elegance.

▲ Aqua walls and opaque aqua glass create a sleek yet glamorous backdrop to pale sycamore wooden kitchen units and glossy granite work-tops for a luxury kitchen that seems almost too beautiful to work in. The added bonus of using safety-thickness glass for splashbacks and tabletops is its easy-clean quality – no dirty grout to scrub. The end result is practical yet chic urban style.

is this the right look for me?

French chic is ideal for you if you:
- ✔ love **elegant, sophisticated** room schemes
- ✔ yearn for a **touch of romance**
- ✔ like **ornate**, beaded, intricate accessories
- ✔ have an **adults-only** home or older children

Avoid if any of the following is true:
- ✘ I need a **kid-proof** home
- ✘ I prefer **strong colours** to create different moods in every room
- ✘ I like **dramatic**, individual décor
- ✘ I hate spending time tidying rooms on a daily basis, so **high-maintenance** looks really aren't my cup of tea
- ✘ I live in a **country** cottage

THE BASICS OF
**FRENCH
CHIC**

COLOUR

French style owes much to the Art Nouveau movement, sharing the same colour schemes and borrowing 1930s influences for period charm. Its sophisticated palette of silvery grey-tinged pastels ranges from icy blue to sage grey-green and dusky mauve. No one colour should ever dominate, so use only harmonious tones in each room for an expensive, elegant look which does not need to shout to achieve a classy end result. Team with softest ivory, oyster or even grey-toned white ceilings to continue the softness of this look, but avoid brilliant white which would be far too harsh.

• Think **pearlescent pastel colours**

TONES LIKE:

- **ivory**
- **palest shell pink**
- **marshmallow pink**
- **dusty lilac**
- **soft thistle**
- **minted apple**
- **bleached topaz**
- **Persian-kitten grey**
- **Wedgwood blue**

TEAM WITH:

- **silver and glass accessories**
- **opulent velvets and silks**
- **shimmering light-reflective finishes**

colour tips

CEILINGS

There is no rule that says ceilings have to be white or cream and this is one style in which softly coloured ceilings work particularly well. To find the perfect shade to match your walls, add a tiny amount of your wall colour to a pot of **soft white** or **ivory** and mix well. This will give just a hint of colour and create a barely there yet perfectly coordinated tone for an infinitely more elegant result.

WOODWORK

Avoid brilliant white at all costs, as it will kill the softness and add a harsh modern note to your beautifully sophisticated room schemes. Choose instead an **ivory** or **pale dove grey**.

ABOVE PICTURE RAILS

If you are lucky enough to have either the original picture rail or a room with a high enough ceiling for you to put one in without it looking out of place, you will be able to add a fourth colour to tone with your main section of wall, woodwork and ceiling. Since subtle colour layering is key to this look, this is obviously a definite bonus. Generally, the rule is to opt for a paler version of the colour on your walls, and then go paler again on your ceiling for a sophisticated blended effect. However, if you want to be more adventurous you can go for another colour above the picture rail, as long as this is the shade you choose to blend on to your ceiling in a lighter form.

WALLS

Sleek and sophisticated, French chic demands walls in muted tones and quiet finishes to form a subtle backdrop rather than be a feature in their own right. Matt-painted walls suit perfectly but pearlescent paints used in small doses magnify the light and airy mood.

Unless you opt for a panelled look, aim for completely smooth and totally unblemished finishes for your walls. Matt paints intensify the powdery effect of the French colour palette and should form your dominant choice, but silk emulsion or even pearlescent paint used in limited areas is a wonderful way to add glamorous shimmer and a light-reflective quality to areas worthy of focus, such as a chimney breast. Subtle silver or gold gilding to highlight mouldings can be striking and adds to the air of luxury.

◄ **Toile-de-Jouy wallpaper is a traditional option for a highly feminine version of the French look. Rural scenes of people and sometimes cherubs or angels are the most common toile-de-Jouy images, always in a two-tone pen and ink-style print.**

▲ **Matt-finish ceramic wall tiles add sophistication when used as a splashback in a kitchen or bathroom. Here plain ceramic tiles in four delicately muted shades are mixed for subtle pattern and interest to enhance a kitchen.**

◀ **Pastel emulsions with a grey or silvery base give a sophisticated touch to any room, from muted dove grey or lavender to silvery sage green and duck-egg blue.** Surprisingly, both powdery lime-wash styles of paint finish and soft-sheen emulsions work, but choose one or the other to use throughout your home for consistency.

▶ **Here rectangular tiles have been laid in the fashion of bricks, as was popular in the 1920s and 1930s, for a look that is much softer than we are used to today.** Teamed with modern copies of the 1930s-style square pedestal basin and a double-ended or roll-top bath, the look is complete.

◀ **Panelling with intricate mouldings creates the ornate, aged effect that is in keeping with this theme and can be fitted to dado or picture-rail height depending on your taste.** It is ideal for period properties but is best avoided in a newly built home, where it will look merely fake and contrived. It is relatively simple to recreate this look by fixing planed timber or **MDF** battening to walls (you could ask a carpenter to do this for you) and painting it all one shade for a sophisticated finish.

F LOORS

This essentially sensual style of decorating requires flooring choices that both look and feel luxurious – so take off your shoes and choose with your toes as well as your eyes. Mixing smooth tiles with softest deep-pile carpet will excite the senses as you move from room to room.

Glossy marbles, sumptuous velvet or saxony carpets, sleek marquetry flooring and chic creamy limestone all appeal to both the eye and the naked foot, and although they are undoubtedly at the top end of the price range, they are a joy to behold. Fakes are acceptable, but only top-quality choices – cheap vinyls will definitely not do. Beauty takes precedence over practicality every time for French chic room schemes, so you would be wise to think carefully before decorating all but the most immaculate family home.

◀ **Limestone comes in a range of creamy tones and is ideal for creating a very sophisticated-looking floor that blends in with, rather than dominates, a scheme. However, it does need sealing and regular maintenance to protect it against damage, and its porous nature means it is best avoided in family bathrooms.**

▲ **If you want softness you can really sink your toes into, luxurious velour or velvet saxony carpets make a wonderful flooring choice, especially for the bedroom. Look out for cream or pastel shades in keeping with your overall colour scheme.**

▸ Ideal for bedrooms, living rooms, large hallways and dining rooms, oriental silk rugs in pastel hues fit this look surprisingly well. They hint at wealth and privilege and a well-travelled background – an illusion every Parisian would like to promote, regardless of actual lifestyle. Cut-pile rather than flat-weave rugs are the best option and look fabulous on wood or marble floors.

◂ Perfect for a classic, slightly retro look in a hallway or 1930s-style bathroom, crisp black and white tiles laid on the diagonal make a chic choice. Look out for marble-effect tiles with subtle veining for the maximum sense of opulence underfoot.

▸ Super-sleek wood or laminate flooring is incredibly flexible to use and suitable for most rooms (except the bathroom or kitchen, where humidity can be a problem). This makes it ideal for French style, as the aim is to use the same flooring throughout your home for continuity. This chic cherry hardwood is perfect.

FABRICS

Think grandeur, faded elegance and opulent texture to guide you to the right fabrics. Despite the sophisticated and subdued colour palette, Parisian-style fabrics are the height of decadence in terms of their sensuous quality and tactile appeal.

Thick-pile velvets and snuggly chenilles add instant depth and richness to sofa upholstery and even curtaining, and look magnificent in silvery-tinged shades that appear to change colour depending on your light source – natural, lamp or candle. Silks and satins add the perfect textural contrast with their light-reflective sheen, so use them on scatter cushions, bedspreads, padded headboards and even an over-bed tester-style canopy for an opulent note that Marie Antoinette herself would approve of. Then look out for

shimmering organzas and voiles for a glittering, layered look and a chic alternative to nets at your windows. Finally, remember that pattern is generally best kept to a minimum, with toile-de-Jouy the favourite option but still used in relatively small doses. Beading and hand-embroidery are also pretty ways to build on these delicate schemes. For a more modern twist you could also consider using smooth suede, fluffy flokati or sheepskin-style material for cushions and rugs.

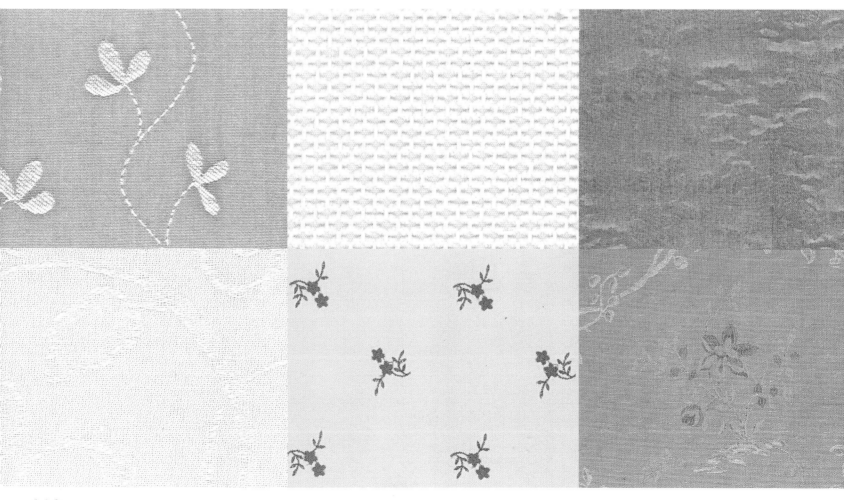

◀ **Self-patterned fabrics** in which the pattern is highlighted only in certain lights offer a sophisticated way to add a more ornate look. Sketchy floral prints, including toile-de-Jouy, are authentic to 18th-century French style. Choose either or both fabrics for larger areas of upholstery for an elegant yet restrained patterned effect.

▶ **Light-reflective satins** and silks make a wonderful choice for cushions, upholstery and curtaining. In particular look out for those that appear to have a two-tone quality and therefore change colour depending on the lighting or where you view them from. Used sparingly, this need not be a costly option. Here the seat top of a blanket box has been recovered for instant glamour at low cost.

◀ **Furry rugs** underfoot add to the sense of luxury. Sheepskin – even pastel dyed – would work. Fake fur could be used as a trim for a floral eiderdown for extra opulence, but would work just as well on a single cushion cover.

KITCHEN

Forget rustic French café style and think instead of a top city restaurant for the sense of sophistication this room needs. Sleek good looks and uncluttered practical layout are far more important here than space for relaxation or family get-togethers.

Seek out kitchen units with rounded edges and minimal detailing on the door fronts for a streamlined, unfussy look. Glossy laminate finishes in white or pastel tones work beautifully, as do pale woods like cherry, maple, pear or the slightly less sophisticated birch. Door handles tend to be of sensuous curved silver metal, to appeal to the sense of touch. Glossy-textured finishes extend also to work-tops, which look incredibly expensive in Corian®, marble, sealed limestone or slick granite – or, of course, a modern fake, which would cost a fraction of the real thing. Walls should be pale, preferably in matt emulsion. Lilac and aqua tones work well to add muted contrast to light wood units. They also help to create a more spacious feel thereby minimizing the impact of general kitchen clutter. To finish, choose steel, brushed-aluminium, white or pastel-toned appliances which blend seamlessly into the scheme rather than shout 'high-tech'.

kitchen **essentials**

- ✔ marble or **granite-effect** work-tops
- ✔ flush kitchen doors in pale wood or **glossy laminates**
- ✔ wood or **limestone floors**
- ✔ **silvery appliances**, including a modern range
- ✔ crisp but unobtrusive **recessed ceiling lighting**
- ✔ high-tech **coffee machine** on display

▼ **Slick appliances in mirror-like stainless steel or brushed aluminium suit this style of kitchen perfectly. A range cooker is the ultimate choice, although you could consider a cream Aga if you want to add a touch of period style. Even a standard built-in oven looks infinitely more urban in a silver finish.**

▶ **Sleek laminate flooring or limestone is ideal for this kitchen décor, but if you need something slightly more low maintenance, look out for pale stone fakes in large-tile sizes to create a spacious feel.**

▾ Sophisticated wood units give the urban Parisian kitchen a look of pure luxury, as well as reflecting light to maximize the feeling of space. Long-length, sleek brushed-silver handles make a statement and are surprisingly practical to use, although not ideal at child-head height because of their sharpish ends. Shiny white ceramic tiles and a black granite-look work-top complete the uncluttered room.

▴ Attention to detail is apparent even down to the smallest appliance. This curvacious, retro-style toaster is the ideal, especially in a pretty pastel tone.

▾ Slate, black granite or manmade Corian® work-tops in a malachite tone add contrast to a predominantly pale colour scheme. Cool to the touch, they are incredibly durable and will never go out of fashion. If you cannot afford the real thing, there are some wonderful manmade copies on the high street, or opt for pale wood laminates in pear or maple instead.

LIVING ROOM

Creating a genteel atmosphere in which to relax and entertain should be your aim with this room. It is the ideal space in which to experiment with luxurious fabrics, larger-than-life mirrors, crystal-drop lighting and a fluffy rug underfoot.

Best of all, because it needs to be understated rather than overpoweringly ornate, you do not need to spend enormous sums to set the scene. Junk shops and architectural salvage yards are marvellous hunting grounds for unusual accessories. Look out for gilded picture frames you could revamp as eye-catching mirrors. Or, if that fails, treat yourself to an authentic Venetian glass mirror with an etched floral frame to sit above an impressive marble or limestone-effect fireplace. A stunning chaise-longue in delicate damask or even velvet upholstery will capture the look perfectly. Many high-street stores now stock designs that would suit, not to mention striking chandeliers, too. A Louis XVI sofa is the most authentic choice, if you can find one at a price to suit. Then finish off with sleek wooden flooring, delicate lighting and scent to evoke an elegant feminine mood.

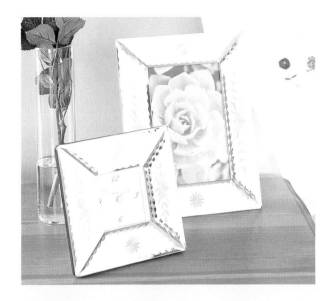

▲ **Venetian glass is a beautifully decorative choice, not just for wall mirrors but candle sconces and picture frames, too.**

living room essentials

- ✔ **crystal chandelier**
- ✔ **Louis XVI-style sofa** or armchair, or a chaise-longue
- ✔ bolster-style **silk cushions** at each end of your sofa
- ✔ silver or gold ornate **over-mantel mirror**
- ✔ embroidered silk or **fluffy sheepskin** or flokati rug

▶ **Chaises-longues immediately add a romantic period note to both living rooms and bedrooms. Look for those with sumptuous upholstery in velvet, chenille or silky damask.**

▲ Crystal chandeliers with glittering droplets and lustrous metallic finishes are a wonderful choice to adorn any Parisian-style room. Even if it is the only ornate accessory you add, it will bring the room to life. What is more, you do not need to spend a fortune – a good high-street alternative can do the job just as well as any crystal original.

▲ Sugared-almond pastel colours on walls, floors and furniture give this room a soft and elegant feel without being overtly 'girly'. The sofa seen here is much more contemporary than might be expected, but because it is pale pink and surrounded with French chic-style details, from the large ornate mirror to the patterned wallpaper, it echoes the look in a very accessible way.

▶ A pretty scrolled side table adds interest to an alcove or sofa end. This charming design is made in metal and has been given a slightly distressed paint finish for an aged yet elegant look.

BEDROOM

Mystery, romance and comfort are core to the French boudoir. This room needs to feel like an elegant cosy haven where you could lie in bed all day – whatever the reality. Indulge yourself with dreamy colours for walls and linens, add floaty curtaining and lots of delicate accessories.

The bed always takes centre stage and is a lavish affair, being either an ornate silver or white-enamelled bedstead with scrolled headboard and base, or a bateau-lit, which is basically a mattress surrounded entirely by rich cognac-toned wood with a headboard and base that curve out at either end. The other option is simply to revamp a fairly ordinary divan with a glamorous silk or velvet padded headboard. The way you add sheeting and blankets to your bed is also important. The French do not 'make' their beds in the morning, they 'dress' them. Layers of soft linen sheets topped with a silk-covered eiderdown and then the plumpest of feather-filled pillows would be authentic. If you feel you must cheat with a striking duvet, do at least add tiny dress cushions and a bedspread draped at the foot of the bed for a more French feel. Finally, no bedroom in this scheme would

bedroom **essentials**

✔ **ornate armoire** in whitewashed paint finish
✔ **dressing table and stool**, plus three-way mirror
✔ **crystal-droplet** wall or bedside lights
✔ **silk or satin bedspread** and cushions
✔ metal **scrolled bedstead** or bedhead – preferably silver or white
✔ folding fabric-covered **bedroom screen**

be complete without an ornate dressing table at which to sit and do your make-up and hair. Choose a three-sectioned vanity mirror for authenticity.

▼ **Chaises-longues suggest romantic liaisons and are perfect for this style of bedroom. Choose one with velvet or damask upholstery and pile high with cushions to enhance the luxurious image.**

▶ **A Venetian glass mirror is the ultimate choice for a French dressing table – perfect for pampering nights in or getting ready for glamorous nights out. No one could fail to feel a little more beautiful staring into one of these. If you cannot afford the real thing, look for reproductions, which cost much less.**

◄ With its delicate pastel lilac colour scheme, antique-effect armoire and delicate wrought-iron bedstead, this bedroom epitomizes the sophisticated elements essential to the French chic bedroom. The light and airy scheme would suit almost any home and is relatively easy to put together with high-street and junk-shop finds.

▼ Create interest in a bland corner of the room with a delicately carved wooden chair with exquisite silk-print upholstery – or a brilliant fake with a sophisticated flower motif.

BATHROOM

Candlelit bubble baths instantly spring to mind when imagining the ultimate Parisian bathroom. This is not a place merely to wash and get clean, it is a sanctuary in which to luxuriate, a pamper zone in which to relax and enjoy yourself … preferably with a glass of wine!

In an ideal world, a roll-top bath would be the ultimate accessory, but a roomy double-ended design would work, too. Just treat yourself to a classic bath/shower mixer tap for a touch of period charm. Floors are usually tiled and sleek underfoot, which contrasts sensuously with the fluffiest of bath towels and mats, but marble-effect vinyl will at least look the part if cash is tight or your floor will not take the weight. Retro brick-style tiles are a wonderful choice for walls while a 1930s-style basin and globe-style wall lights will make reference to the Art Nouveau influences. There are plenty of well-priced reproductions around to cheat the effect for less.

▸ **An all-cream colour scheme with sleek textures such as marble floor tiles and a limestone fireplace give this bathroom a wonderful sense of space, while candlelight adds instant romantic atmosphere. This adults-only bathroom captures all the essentials of Parisian style without making an overt theme statement and the roll-top bath gives that essential element of period style and romance.**

bathroom essentials

✔ freestanding roll-top or roomy **double-ended bath**
✔ classic **washstand basin** with integral metal towel rail
✔ **ornate mirror** with a light either side
✔ **chair** if you have space
✔ Egyptian cotton towels and a huge **fluffy dressing gown**
✔ period-style bath/shower **mixer tap**

▸ **This ornate pedestal-legged ceramic basin will suit the theme wonderfully if you have the space. Part basin, part vanity unit, it is the perfect place to display your perfumes and other luxurious toiletries for a very feminine feel.**

◂ Luxurious bathing demands the largest, fluffiest towels to wrap up in and dry yourself after a relax in the deepest of bubble baths, so splash out and make this room a real comfort zone. Find space for a chair where you can sit and pamper yourself with creams and lotions.

▴ Glass jars make perfect storage for soaps and cotton wool. Soaps in individual wrappers add to the sense of hotel-style luxury for a really sensuous indulgent bathroom scheme.

▾ Make a display of elegant toiletries, such as bath oils, crystals and aromatic candles on an open shelf to continue the sensual mood. Choose colours to suit your scheme. You can always decant high-street bubble baths into chic bottles once the expensive stuff runs out.

MEDITERRANEAN STYLE 6

6 MEDITERRANEAN STYLE

Add an instant summer flavour to any room with the sun-drenched shades and relaxed décor style of the Mediterranean. This look has many crossovers with English country style, making it a wonderful choice for older properties as well as any informal family home.

The key to Mediterranean style is earthy
rusticity. This look is designed for practical comfort and so is relatively cheap to imitate. Of course, the Mediterranean area encompasses many countries and nationalities, but here we are focusing on general style ideas that take their inspiration from Greece and Italy. Look for durability and handmade charm when choosing Mediterranean-inspired furniture. Chunky pine or carved oak items with minimal upholstery are ideal. Aged oak is the most popular wood, but there are lots of warm-toned woodstains, such as honey and richer cognac, that will give living and dining rooms a more sophisticated feel. Wrought iron or polished iron detailing is also commonly used for furniture legs and shelving supports in the Italian home to give a more ornate look. Open storage units, such as baker's rack shelving, can be found in almost any room and hand-painted earthenware is often on display. Both Italian and Greek pottery feature lemon and vine motifs, often in cobalt blue, zingy yellow and jade greens. Look out for rush seats on dining and occasional chairs to add casual charm and the odd tile-topped coffee or console table to add a splash of colour. If you have the opportunity to take a holiday in the Mediterranean you will find it almost impossible to return home without some lovely object to bring authenticity to your scheme.

▲ This cosy family room shows how bold colour is combined with minimal pattern to create a relaxed, informal environment and a distinctly rustic mood. The wrought-iron daybed is a staple for many Mediterranean homes, while the soft colourwash on the walls creates a textured, sun-drenched feel.

◀ Rich terracotta tiles used on the walls to dado height add a warm, inviting mood to this otherwise highly practical bathroom. The shower cubicle is given greater prominence than the bath – as is in keeping with Mediterranean style.

▾ Open, easy-access storage is a common feature of the Mediterranean kitchen, which tends to combine dressers with waist-height units to avoid the fully-fitted look.

key characteristics

- **Chunky pine or battered oak** furniture mixed with occasional **wrought-iron pieces** such as open shelving units.

- **Slatted window shutters** and floaty muslin drapes to let in lots of sunlight.

- **Earthenware crockery** for everyday use and display.

- Fresh yet simple seashore-inspired colour schemes for **Greek-style** and rich earthy colours for **Italian-style** rooms.

- **Rush-seated chairs**, particularly in the dining room or as occasional chairs in the bedroom.

- **Naïve embroidery** on cushions and bedlinen.

- **Handmade heavy lace** used as dining-table runners and to trim cushion covers and pillowcases.

- **Whitewashed wooden** floorboards or terracotta- or ceramic-tiled floors.

is this **the right look** for me?

Mediterranean style is ideal for you if you:

✔ like the idea of a permanent **holiday mood** at home

✔ prefer laid-back, **informal** interiors

✔ want an uncluttered, **non-flowery** version of country style

✔ live in an **older property**

✔ have rooms that receive **lots of light**

Avoid if any of the following is true:

✗ I think **soft fabric textures** and pretty curtaining are essential

✗ My home is on the **cold and dark** side

✗ I could never have **tiled floors** in any room

✗ I hate **pine** and **wrought-iron** furniture

COLOUR

Holidays and trips abroad provide boundless inspiration for this decorative colour palette, so take your camera and snap away. There are plenty of options to allow you to create a different mood in each room of your home. For crisp, fresh room schemes that seem filled with light, the clean tones of the Greek colour palette are ideal. The Italian colour palette, being much richer and earthier, is better for cosy yet sophisticated schemes.

greek style

Just imagine whitewashed villas covered in pink bougainvillaea, azure skies, turquoise seas and the vibrant yellow sun and you have the Greek palette. There are not many colours to choose from but rather shades of the essential sparkling tones of sea, sun and sky, with a few vivid contrasts such as hot pink and citrus shades thrown in. Together they will create light, airy and invigorating schemes that guarantee a summer flavour all year round in rooms that receive a fair amount of natural daylight.

• Think **sea and sunshine** shades

TONES LIKE:

brilliant white

citrus yellow

sky blue

crisp cobalt

hot pink

spearmint green

TEAM WITH:

•   **white-glossed floorboards**
•   **lime-washed furniture**
•   **rough-plastered walls**
•   **wicker and rush seating**

colour tips

- **Aim to feature** no more than three colours in any room on walls, floors and furniture and you'll be halfway to capturing the simple naïve décor that epitomizes much of Mediterranean style.
- **Italian décor can** be made more sophisticated with tonal layers of similar shades but only if you want to create a city feel as opposed to a more rustic country theme.
- **Brilliant white is essential** for walls, especially in the Grecian home which uses this as a crisp backdrop for the zingy colour palette shown in the form of soft furnishings and accessories. Soft whites or ivories simply cannot compete for the same fresh, sun-drenched feel.

italian style

The sun-drenched shades that give this palette its rich, warm appeal are taken directly from nature. Fields of golden corn, sunflowers, dark green cypress trees, lemons, vines and olive trees make up the Italian landscape and the same colours appear on house exteriors, too, creating a harmonious palette of softly toning shades. All lend themselves to both rustic room schemes and a more sophisticated look. Plus they are perfect for homes that lack character or warmth and tend to be on the darker side, and for anyone who wants to conjure up an inviting, intimate mood.

- Think **rich, earthy** shades

TONES LIKE:

cream

golden corn

sunflower yellow

burnt red

terracotta

olive green

bottle green

TEAM WITH:

- **terracotta-tiled floors**
- **murals on walls**
- **rustic aged pine or oak furniture with wrought-iron detailing**

WALLS

Matt and textured finishes are the authentic choices for the Mediterranean-style home. You would certainly never find wallpaper or fussy panelling in this sort of environment except in high-class hotels. Modern paints allow you to fake the look without long-term commitment.

Greek style is by far the most simplistic of the two looks with white walls predominating throughout the entire house. Italian homes tend to mix a greater variety of textures from mosaic-tiled splashbacks to glazed colourwashes and even murals reminiscent of religious frescos. Tiling is an absolute essential in the somewhat utilitarian and practical bathrooms, and often the same tile design is used to cover both floors and a good percentage of walls, too. And rough plaster can be used to add texture to interior walls throughout the home.

◀ **Mosaic tiling, most commonly seen on Mediterranean floors, can work brilliantly on walls, too, for example as a splashback in a kitchen or to dado height in a hallway. Here a variety of matt, stone-coloured terrazzo-style tiles have been applied to create a delicate and sophisticated fake panel effect.**

▲ **Rough textures, from rough plaster to Artex, emphasize the rustic simplicity of this scheme, helping to create an informal and totally unpolished look. This is a great way to add character and has the advantage of turning difficult bumpy walls into a positive style statement.**

◄ Colourwashed paint effects help fake the look of rough-textured walls without making the same commitment. In addition, they create an opaque layered glaze that is wonderful for reflecting more light and mimics the look of Italian frescos to perfection. Choose shades of ochre, terracotta and umber, layering one at a time over a base coat of cream or sand for a warming end result.

▲ Bare brick walls also suit this look in small doses, as on an over-hearth wall or kitchen chimney breast for a charming raw quality.

◄ Ceramic tiles cover most of the walls in Italian bathrooms and feature in Greek and Spanish homes, too, as splashbacks. Seek out hand-painted patterns or hand-colourwashed finishes to capture the look.

FLOORS

Mediterranean homes often have just one or two choices of flooring running throughout which creates a wonderful sense of continuity and visual flow from room to room. It also makes for the most practical and low-maintenance option.

Tiled floors are the number one choice

particularly in warm terracotta tones and matt ceramic, although you will find glossier marble appearing in more sophisticated Italian settings. They are easy to clean but have the drawback of being a little too cool underfoot in less sunnier climes of the Northern Hemisphere. However, this can be rectified with the addition of underfloor heating (not as expensive as you might think) and cotton dhurrie-style rugs with a non-slip backing. It is of course possible to cheat the tiled effect with hard vinyl and even laminated flooring which are both warmer, yet still low maintenance. But do avoid cushioned vinyls which mimic but never really fool the viewer, as they will simply look cheap used in large expanses. Soft carpets, such as saxony or velour, have no part to play in the Mediterranean home but if you must have carpet look out for neutral tones and textured designs which echo the finish of natural floor coverings, like coir or sisal, instead.

◄ **Marble mosaics are the sophisticated Mediterranean choice for schemes that hint at Roman heritage. You can use one-tone tiles or a selection of colours to make more ornate patterns for a really eye-catching floor – in an entrance hall, for instance. This charming fish motif is one example that would fit perfectly in a bathroom.**

▶ **Natural-fibre flooring suits the earthy feel of the Mediterranean home. Rush matting and sisal or seagrass carpeting will give a durable finish, but you may find them rough for bare feet. As fitted carpets are a rarity, choose a large rug to cover all but a border round the edge of the room.**

◄ Terracotta tiles have a warm country appearance that tones beautifully with the Mediterranean colour palette, particularly more Italian and Spanish looks. You will find them most commonly in kitchens and hallways, although some Mediterranean villas use them throughout the entire house for continuity. In colder climes, underfloor heating would be a major benefit.

◄ Ceramic tiles are another great option. For a rustic finish, consider something like these hand-painted encaustic tiles in an entrance hall. It is also common to use tiles on bathroom floors, but choose matt or ribbed versions for a non-slip finish for safety.

▶ White-glossed floorboards are a cheap yet surprisingly durable and easy-clean option, and of course the all-white finish reflects maximum light. Teamed with all-white walls, the floor appears to blend in seamlessly to further increase the sense of space. Adding natural wood accents lends a note of warmth to the scheme. This look is perfect if you are aiming for a Greek feel.

FABRICS

Fabrics and soft furnishings are surprisingly sparse, particularly in rural Mediterranean homes, and tend to be for practical rather than decorative purposes. Fabric appears on cushions, sofa covers and bedlinens and in the kitchen. Curtaining is rare as most homes use shutters instead.

Crisp white cotton is key to both Greek and Italian homes especially in the bedrooms where beds tend to be dressed with little other than fresh sheets and perhaps a white embroidered bedspread. Lace is also incredibly popular, not the filigree netting style of French and English homes but a chunky, hand-woven almost crocheted effect in cream, ivory and soft white. The Mediterraneans use it to cover cushions and drape across tables or use as a simple runner over a dresser or chest of drawers for a note of

prettiness – to be authentic you should use it in only minimal amounts to avoid a twee look. Coloured and patterned fabrics feature on sofa upholstery and table linens but only in limited amounts. Durable cottons and linens are most popular in plains, stripes and checks but floral designs are rare. Anything that tones with the colour palettes on pages 124–5 will work in this scheme. One last alternative is hand-embroidered finishes using rather large, naïve stitching in thick thread to decorative effect.

◂ **Soft citrus-inspired shades** are lovely in an Italian-themed home, adding a sunny glow that tones perfectly with, for example, terracotta flooring.

▴ **Handmade lace** is a common feature of homes across the Mediterranean. You find it used for tablecloths, bedlinens and runners over a chest of drawers.

◂ **Simple, chunky embroidery** adds a charming homespun quality to bedlinens and cushions. Here a cream thread on taupe linen is a good example of the subtle way it is used.

mediterranean style 131

KITCHEN

Cooking and eating are taken incredibly seriously, with mealtimes forming the basis of any number of convivial get-togethers. Communal cooking sessions are not uncommon and can last for hours so it is no wonder that these kitchens tend to be spacious, practical and relaxed.

The image of the kitchen as 'heart of the home' fits this décor style more aptly than any other in this book. As the centre of activity for many families, this room is generally well planned and very spacious. Storage includes a combination of freestanding cupboards, wall-hung shelves and utensil racks for open, easy access to pots, pans, herbs and so on. Terracotta tiles complete the charmingly aged, country mood. Look out for rattan and wrought-iron finishes on tables, chairs and baker's rack style dressers for an Italian themed kitchen. Rush seating on chairs is a common detail for a rustic Greek feel. Then invest in crisp white table linens and chunky earthenware china in colourful glazes for serving and everyday display.

▶ Placing a table centrally like this emphasizes the importance of the Mediterranean kitchen for family gatherings. Dark wood furniture gives the room a rich feel but is kept informal by teaming it with rustic wicker, practical terracotta flooring and simple chunky earthenware rather than delicate china. Wrought-iron detailing on the chairs and rush seating also add to a more country mood.

kitchen essentials

- ✔ freestanding **butcher's block** or central island work-top
- ✔ **butler's sink**
- ✔ freestanding kitchen units in rustic wood or with **distressed paint finishes** for a fake aged effect
- ✔ open wooden or **painted dresser**
- ✔ **terracotta glazed** oven-to-tableware
- ✔ naïve hand-painted **earthenware** crockery

▶ This wrought-iron and rattan baker's rack would sit comfortably in any room but provides informal storage in a kitchen.

◀ Keeping herbs close to hand draws attention again to the importance of food and cooking in Mediterranean style. Here colourful food tins have been reused as plant holders for a highly individual touch.

▴ Tiled dining tables add an instant Mediterranean feel. Practical and easy to clean, they also look particularly attractive if you opt for hand-painted tiles featuring lemons, other fruit and vine motifs like the ones in this Italian-inspired design.

▾ Butler's sinks are a popular option, but here a soft yellow manmade sink adds a sunny note to give a modern Mediterranean flavour instead.

LIVING ROOM

Wooden-framed sofas with legs and frame on display are the authentic option for this room scheme, but you can still recreate a similar style using completely upholstered seating provided you mix in more rustic wooden furniture to echo the theme.

Chunky pine or battered oak is the best choice for coffee tables, bookcases and console tables, although wrought-iron detailing can be used to suggest Italian influence. A baker's rack bookcase fits the look perfectly and is ideal for displaying hand-painted earthenware treasures. Floaty muslin panels set off the windows to perfection, although in colder climes you could disguise weightier curtains or blinds behind for added warmth. Wooden slatted window shutters are a must, particularly at full-length patio doors, but if your budget does not stretch that far you could always try hinged louvre doors instead. Many Mediterranean living rooms incorporate a dining area, too, in an open-plan through-room layout.

living room **essentials**

- ✔ **chunky pine** coffee table
- ✔ terracotta floor tiles or **whitewashed floorboards**
- ✔ **wood-burning stove** or fake alternative
- ✔ **coloured** muslin curtains
- ✔ **wooden-framed sofa** with loose seat and back cushions and legs on show
- ✔ cotton **dhurrie-style** rug

◀ **Net curtains would be completely wrong at Mediterranean-style windows, so here, rather than opt for stark shutters, a half-length panel of embroidered fabric has been used to give privacy and filter light.**

▶ **Adding texture is essential to stop this décor style looking too bare, as this wicker armchair shows. Other attractive additions would be rustic woven baskets or a roughly woven cotton rug.**

◄ Blue glass adds vibrancy to a Greek-themed room and the mosaic, although not strictly authentic, is very effective. Terracotta flowerpots painted with matt white emulsion stand out well against blue walls and are easy to copy.

▾ Here wicker textures, whitewashed floorboards and floaty muslin curtains have been teamed with a rather traditional English-style upholstered sofa to apc the Mediterranean look without sacrificing comfort. Sky-blue walls add a fresh feel and contrast beautifully with citrus yellow curtaining.

BEDROOM

Decorated simply with a chunky wooden or wrought-iron bedstead, freestanding wardrobe and dressing table, the Mediterranean bedroom can look a little sparse. Tiled or sanded floorboards offer no additional softness so add charm with embroidered linen, lace or wall-hung plates.

Keeping cool and ensuring that everything is easy to clean are the main priorities here, and the look has a definite rustic charm that will soon win you over. Crisp cotton sheets, with a simply embroidered or patchwork bedspread, are really all you need to dress the bed for a Greek or a more pared-back, Italian country theme. Fussy details are quite out of place, but if you feel the need to soften the scheme with accessories, consider hanging a bedspread on the wall, displaying the odd painted plate and decorating a corner of the room with a simple ceramic washstand and water jug. Curtains are much less common than window shutters, although Italian city homes and hotels may feature them in subdued floral prints.

bedroom essentials

✔ **wrought-iron** or wooden bedstead
✔ cotton sheets and **simple** bedlinen
✔ **window shutters**
✔ minimal furniture, including a large wooden wardrobe and **vanity unit** with drawers
✔ wooden **rush-seated** or metal occasional chair

◄ **Window shutters rather than fussy curtains or blinds are the norm and add an instant holiday flavour to any room. Exterior shutters that can be pulled over the window from inside are authentic on the Continent but recessed windows may feature interior shutters instead, which are an easier look to recreate. Perforated shutters such as these offer privacy without blocking out all light if you prefer to be woken by the sun.**

▲ **A chunky freestanding wooden wardrobe is by far the most appropriate choice for this style. Dark rich cognac wood tones like the one shown suit Italian bedrooms, while Greek looks will benefit from a beaten or antique pine or lime-washed oak wardrobe design instead.**

◄ Wrought-iron or polished iron furniture adds an Italianate influence to any room. This sophisticated console table features a trailing grapevine motif which echoes the Mediterranean influence.

▲ An all-neutral colour scheme gives this bedroom a tranquil feel but is prevented from looking too sophisticated by the choice of a rustic stone flagged floor. Accessories and decorative detail are kept to an absolute minimum to maintain the earthy country mood.

BATHROOM

Practical if somewhat utilitarian, the typical Mediterranean bathroom is designed purely for cleansing in a cool environment rather than for relaxation. Low-maintenance, easy-clean surfaces and wall-hung sanitary ware are common to both Greek and Italian homes.

A large shower enclosure always takes precedence over a bath, and a bidet is an essential rather than an optional extra. Tiled walls and floors have a dual purpose, being cool to the touch and ultra-hygienic because they are easy to clean. If you want to complete the look properly, look for waffle-textured European-style towels and bath mats. They are a little less soft to the touch than loop-pile towels, but soak up water far more efficiently.

▲ This cabinet was given a distressed paint finish for an aged effect, to suit Greek style. To copy, simply paint a dark colour over a lighter colour and sand back areas of natural wear and tear.

bathroom **essentials**

- ✔ **walk-in shower** enclosure
- ✔ tiled walls and floor, in **white ceramic**
- ✔ **wall-hung suite**, including a bidet
- ✔ chrome wall-hung heated **towel rail**
- ✔ Monobloc **mixer taps** on bath and basin
- ✔ Continental-style **waffle-textured** towels
- ✔ good **storage** to hide away clutter

◄ **Rich olive-green and pale yellow tones give this bathroom an Italian flavour. The lack of tiles is uncommon but shows how easily the look can be adapted for a more cosy feel.**

▶ **Hand-painted tiles add charm and prettiness when used in small doses, such as for a splashback for a basin. These simple white, yellow and blue motif tiles are similar to the sort found in any Mediterranean bathroom store.**

▲ Two-tone tiles in soft azure and warming terracotta prevent this practical bathroom from looking minimalist and capture the look of a sophisticated Greek-style setting. A urinal is a distinctly European bathroom feature. You could fake the look of shutters at a window with louvre doors bought through any good **DIY** store.

◄ Wall-hung sanitary ware is a practical choice. The design ensures all pipework is hidden from view in boxed-in support units keeping cleaning to a minimum. The added bonus is that it also frees up floor space, which gives a more roomy feel.

SCANDINAVIAN STYLE

7 SCANDINAVIAN STYLE

Fresh and pretty without being fussy, Scandinavian style crosses both modern and traditional tastes. Its airy colours are the perfect choice for maximizing a sense of light and space in any home. Northern hemisphere properties lacking natural daylight will benefit most as they share a similar blue natural light to Scandinavia.

Originating in Norway, Finland and especially Sweden, this clean, crisp style was developed as a way of bringing light and brightness into northern hemisphere homes that suffer from a shortage of daylight throughout the long winter months. Little wonder then that white is the essential base colour for every room. Today, Scandinavian style and what you can buy in Ikea, are seen as one and the same thing: high fashion, with streamlined light wood furnishings for a strong contemporary look. Yet traditionalists, too,

will find something to interest them in Scandinavian décor, which takes a certain amount of inspiration from the ornate 18th-century Gustavian period, for example furniture with turned legs and elaborate mouldings. White walls, light-coloured upholstery and pale hard flooring fit both looks, making this the perfect style for rooms where you want to create a really open, spacious feel. Interpret the basic ingredients as you wish and go for either ultra-modern, fresh and clean or pretty, ornate and elegant.

◂ **Eau de nil colour walls teamed with soft gold seating give this room a modern Scandinavian flavour, which seems light and airy without being too cool. A cream, subtly patterned rug softens the floorboards while simple voile curtains add a breezy mood at the large windows.**

▾ A delicate hand-painted motif gives the kitchen dining table a pretty feminine feel and contrasts with stripy roman blinds and a few choice pieces of gingham crockery to add subtle pattern to a delicate grey-blue and white scheme. Unfinished wooden chairs with rush seats are treated with a rich aqua-blue woodstain for a deeper layer of colour.

▸ The icy colours and ornately carved furniture in this room echo the traditional, more opulent Gustavian period of Scandinavian interior design. Tall, narrow windows are given a fuss-free finish with simple swagged pelmets, and a panelled effect is painted on to the walls to increase the classically elegant mood.

key characteristics

- White or just off-white walls.

- Pale wood such as birch, white or pale painted furniture.

- Wood, laminate or white-glossed floorboards.

- Streamlined window treatments and floating voiles to let in maximum light.

- A limited colour palette of white, off-white, greys, duck-egg blues plus limited amounts of cherry red as an accent shade.

- Bright lighting and lots of it.

- Open-plan living.

is this **the right look** for me?

Scandinavian style is ideal for you if you:

✔ find the country look appeals but want something **more sophisticated** and less traditional and cluttered

✔ need to **add light** and **brightness** to your home

✔ prefer **light woods** like beech and birch to rich dark or mid-toned varieties

✔ have a **north-facing** or gloomily lit home

✔ want an **elegant** but family-friendly look

Avoid if any of the following is true:

✗ **Cosy carpet** is the only flooring I can live with in my main rooms

✗ Muddy **pet pawprints** are a problem

✗ I need **lots of colour** in my rooms to invigorate me

✗ I like to create **a sense of variety** from room to room

✗ I find **wooden flooring** cold and noisy underfoot

COLOUR

The Scandinavian colour palette has a natural bias towards pale, cool tones. Interior designers know that these shades can create the illusion of walls receding and so help to make a room feel bigger. They are also better reflectors of whatever natural daylight is received, unlike warm cosy shades, which tend to soak up light. You might worry that such shades will create cold, unwelcoming rooms, but this is easily avoided by mixing white with ivory and cream tones which have yellow undertones and adding lots of texture and warm real wood touches in the form of floors and furniture. The cosy flicker of lantern light will also add a yellow glow.

• Think **icy, muted** shades

TONES LIKE:

- **pure white**
- **ivory**
- **taupe**
- **palest chambray**
- **Wedgwood blue**
- **duck-egg blue**
- **mint**
- **frosted fir green**
- **cherry red**

TEAM WITH:

- **silvery and tin accessories**
- **crystal-drop lighting**
- **cream upholstery**
- **blond wood furniture**
- **birch wood floors**

making it work

A limited colour palette makes decorating a Scandinavian-style room fairly easy. Use **pure chalky white** as the base colour, then add layers of **off-white**, **grey**, **silver**, **duck-egg blue** or the occasional accent of **cherry red**, **cobalt blue** or, in more traditional schemes, **forest green**.

Traditional Gustavian schemes tend to be **mostly white** with accents of **blue**, while rural Scandinavian décor features quite heavily stencilled walls and even floors for an altogether more homely look. Modern Scandinavian styles mix white walls with bold accessories and warm wood, but avoid fussy patterns. Woodwork can be **pure white**, **natural wood** if you have natural flooring and even one of the darker accent shades if you opt for stencilled walls.

GO TWO-TONE

For the easiest ever interpretation of Scandinavian style create the simplest two-tone colour scheme in traditional **blue and white** or **red and white**. Using a mix of shades of white from **ivory** to **brilliant white** to **icy blue-white** avoids blandness while the second vibrant accent colour adds freshness and contrast. **Cherry** or **scarlet red** are ideal, while your main **blue** can vary from **fresh cobalt** to **sophisticated sky**. Use subtle pattern on limited amounts of upholstery to introduce this second shade, for example a gingham or sketchy floral cushion cover.

WALLS

Your choice of wall finish will depend on whether you prefer a traditional or a modern take on the Scandinavian theme. Modern rooms demand plain, unfussy finishes – it is hard to beat a simple backdrop of off-white emulsion – while period looks need a touch of pattern and texture.

▾ **Shiplap-style wooden boarding that runs horizontally across the wall is a chic choice for bathrooms or behind a bedhead, for example, to create a feature wall. When you think about Swedish saunas you soon understand the inspiration for this look.**

The most common choice for Scandinavian inspired rooms is plain white or off-white emulsioned walls, which set a clean, fresh, almost minimalist backdrop for furniture and the odd patterned item. For contemporary looks a brilliant white works best, offset by white woodwork so the two blend seamlessly together to form a backdrop for natural pine furniture and more striking silver and glass metal designs. Traditional looks require a softer shade, such as ivory, which can be teamed with ivory satinwood painted

furniture for a more sophisticated period look. Of course, an all-white home could easily become incredibly bland so colour can be introduced, particularly in icy blues, for variety. Panelled walls either to dado or full height set a classic mood and are the main sophisticated alternative to smooth finish walls. Or you could opt for a stencilled motif for a folk art twist on Scandinavian style. Floral vines running in vertical stripes is one of most common ways to use a stencil for a hand-painted wallpaper effect.

▴ **Panelled walls are ideally suited to traditional style rooms where a more formal and elaborate yet elegant look is called for. Here Wedgwood-blue walls have been given an interesting three-dimensional effect with a dado rail and panels beneath. These panels were simply faked with wooden mouldings to create the rectangular outline while an ornate wood tile adds focus to each centre.**

◀ **Large mirrors are an essential accessory in almost every room in the Scandinavian home. For sleek modern schemes, choose unframed panels of** mirror simply attached with unobtrusive mirror screws. For traditional schemes, choose a more opulent gilded frame as shown here.

▲ **Wall-to-floor shelving in all white is a brilliant way to add lots of storage space without dominating a room. This design has been built to frame a window, but it would work equally well on either side of and above a doorway to make best use of limited space. Masses of dark books would kill the effect, so hide clutter in natural or white-painted wicker boxes instead.**

◀ **A pretty stencilled motif adds rustic charm to this kitchen/diner but is kept simple by using cherry red against a cream background. Traditional schemes use stencils to create striped effects or rectangular outlines for a fake panel finish.**

scandinavian style 147

FLOORS

Laminate or real wood flooring is undoubtedly the most common choice – which is not surprising when you consider how densely forested Scandinavian countries are. Think pale and light reflective in your choice of flooring and you can't go far wrong.

Scandinavian floors, like the walls, are merely backdrops to the furniture and soft furnishings rather than features in their own right. Generally you should aim to choose a finish that will blend seamlessly and harmoniously with the rest of the room, and treat the floor as your fifth wall. The range of authentic flooring choices is fairly limited in terms of material, with wood and wood-effect laminate by far and away the most popular choices to run throughout an entire property with few visual breaks. Paler woods are ideal but white-

painted floorboards work, too. In each case you will find they are always softened with an attractive rug or two to avoid blandness and to deaden the click-clack sound of footsteps.

The only room in which wooden flooring is not generally suitable is the bathroom, where humid conditions can cause it to warp. Instead, Scandinavian bathrooms are almost always tiled with pale ceramic tiles often with underfloor heating installed to create that 'steam spa' sensation.

▶ **Soft cotton-weave rugs are the primary choice for adding softness and a greater sense of warmth to wooden flooring, although a non-slip underside is obviously essential for safety. This charming diamond-motif rug in delicately subdued hues of grey-blues and creams tones perfectly with the walls and pulls all the colour elements together rather than adding new drama in its own right. Two-tone check rugs in blue and white, green and ivory, or red and white, are also very common.**

◄ Laminate or real wood flooring is often used throughout an entire home, including the kitchen, with no obvious visual breaks. It has two invaluable qualities for this style. First, the rich wood tones add warmth to the pale, sometimes icy colour schemes, and second, the sheen of the finish is excellent for reflecting light around a room. Pale wood finishes, such as natural pine, birch and beech, are authentic choices, but avoid any wood with a red tinge.

▼ Sleek ceramic tiles in a limestone or white finish are a durable, low maintenance choice for kitchens and bathrooms and light reflective too.

▲ Carpet is not at all authentic, but if you prefer the warmth, comfort and lack of noise underfoot it gives, you can cheat and create a light and airy look that retains a Scandinavian flavour by opting for a natural-coloured carpet. Textured weaves can work quite well, as shown here, or opt for a sleek velour or saxony pile in a pale, icy shade to contrast beautifully with white walls for a luxury textured alternative to wood.

FABRICS

The understated elegance of Scandinavian style demands unfussy soft furnishings, so the secret is to put the the emphasis on a restrained use of pattern on cushions and curtains for traditional schemes and choose almost entirely plain fabrics for modern interiors.

The Scandinavians use pattern as a means of introducing a layer of colour to their almost all-white and natural wood surroundings but, as you will already have seen from the colour palette, the choice of tones is kept within strict limits to ensure a simple, sophisticated end result. The size and style of pattern you opt for will depend on whether you prefer a contemporary or traditional look for your home. Bold two-tone checks have a graphic quality suited to more modern rooms, while ginghams look cute and pretty for more rustic, even cottagey looks. Sketchy two-tone floral motifs or stamped-style imagery tend to work best in period settings for a more deliberately grown-up mood. When it comes to texture, cotton is undoubtedly the top choice although sateen finishes, self-patterned damasks and linens also work well. Voiles and muslins are another essential choice at windows for floaty curtains that let in maximum light. Avoid high-sheen fabrics and velvets as they feel too fussy and grand for the mood you are aiming to create.

◀ Fresh blues and whites in varying tones give this bedroom a cool and airy mood, and prove that a four-poster bed needn't look dominant and chunky if you dress it in suitably floaty materials. The footstool with a larger stylized foliage print adds a contemporary note to an otherwise traditional theme.

▼ Crisp two-tone checks and ginghams are integral to Scandinavian style and tend to feature in small amounts in dining-chair upholstery, rugs, cushion covers and kitchen linens. They are a wonderful way of injecting colour into any scheme. The most common colourways are cherry red and white, cobalt blue and white, and chambray and white.

◀ For a slightly more modern interpretation of Swedish style, this living room teams characteristically ornate Gustavian-style armchairs with a contemporary upholstered sofa to give an informal scheme. The taupe sofa upholstery and bold highlights of cherry red in selective soft furnishings add warmth to a look that is still relatively pared back.

KITCHEN

Pale birch or white-painted units form the basis of the average Scandinavian kitchen so as to maximize light and create a feeling of space, but for cosier, more traditional looks it is perfectly feasible to choose colourful painted units instead – use the colour palette for guidance.

▼ **Tempered glass-fronted cupboards with internal lighting continue the emphasis on frosty looks but you will need to use them sensibly for storing items that look attractive on display. Plain or simply patterned china and glass-ware are ideal.**

Aim for clean, clutter-free surfaces and streamlined window treatments, such as roman blinds, to help the room feel as open and airy as possible. Installing good halogen recessed lighting is another essential. If you can, squeeze in a dining table, as this is another common Scandinavian kitchen feature. Look out for natural pine-topped tables with white legs, and chairs with rush seats or gingham covers for a modern rustic finish. Alternatively, authentic Gustavian designs with ornately carved backs are ideal for a through kitchen/diner, where you want a more formal, feel. You will not find much pattern in the Scandinavian kitchen, so adding prettiness with limited use of striped, checked or floral two-tone fabrics is a good idea. The end result should be a harmonious, tranquil and yet informal scheme rather than anything too sleek and minimal.

kitchen essentials

- ✔ white or **pale wood units** – look for doors with minimal detailing, such as simple panelled or tongue-and-groove doors with self-coloured knobs or silver door handles
- ✔ recessed **ceiling spotlights**
- ✔ **checked** or **striped fabrics** used for roman blinds, table linen and loose seat covers
- ✔ real wood or pale laminate flooring for an **easy-clean finish** that reflects light back around the room
- ✔ **built-in oven**, preferably in white, cream or even palest blue
- ✔ open shelving for **easy-access storage**

▶ **To give your dining chairs an instant Scandinavian flavour cover them with gingham chair runners. This cherry red and white runner is simply hemmed fabric that has been loosely tied in place with red ribbon to add softness to an unfinished pine chair.**

▾ White tongue-and-groove panelled kitchen units give an informal modern country feel to this kitchen and are prevented from looking too clinical by the addition of cherry-red tiles and warm wood finishes, such as the work-top, shelving and real wood floor. The white oven blends in beautifully and is more homely than high-tech stainless steel alternatives. Open shelving and utensil racks complete the cosy yet pared-back look.

▸ Traditional cream porcelain in a simple yet sophisticated rib pattern is the perfect serving choice for an elegant kitchen or dining room, and is timelessly classic.

153

LIVING ROOM

Freshness is more important here than cosiness, so furnishings are predominantly in light wood or painted white, with mirrors and minimalist artwork on the walls. Choose accessories such as curtain poles and lamp bases in silver rather than yellow-toned metals, although wrought iron is acceptable in very small doses.

▼ **Crisp, clean lighting is essential in every Scandinavian room. This pinpricked lampshade casts golden light around the room, adding warmth and atmosphere. The cream coloured lamp shade and base mean that the lighting blends into the scheme rather than creating a focus.**

Lighting is essential in the Scandinavian home, so you will invariably find lots of options within this room. Table lamps sit at each end of the sofa while a floor-standing lamp will lift a dark corner or create a pool of light for reading. The main ceiling light will almost certainly be a three- or five-armed chandelier with pretty candle bulbs, sometimes naked and sometimes dressed with pale-toned individual shades. Matching wall sconces work, too, and no Scandinavian living room would be complete without candles of some kind on console tables, around the fireplace and in lanterns in the window.

living room essentials

- ✔ white or **palest cream sofa,** preferably with pale wood legs on show
- ✔ birch or beech laminate or real **wood flooring**
- ✔ **wood-burning stove** or ceramic-tiled fire tower in the corner of a room
- ✔ pale wood **coffee table**
- ✔ **white-painted furniture,** be it a bookcase, dresser or chest of drawers
- ✔ **tray table** painted perhaps in duck-egg blue
- ✔ **large mirror** with an ornate silver or white-painted frame

▶ **Ceramic column fireplaces are a dramatic feature of traditional Swedish style and can be found in both bedrooms and living rooms. The wood-burning stove is often situated in a corner to make a neat yet eye-catching focal point in a room.**

▲ **This console table has been given an aged paint-effect finish for an antique look that adds character to an almost all-white scheme. Note the table's turned legs and burnished silver handles, which are characteristic of traditional Gustavian design.**

▼ This pretty, traditional living room features furniture inspired by the Gustavian period of Scandinavian interiors, when ornate wood carving was an essential feature on leggy armchairs and sofas. The pale colour scheme and lack of heavy upholstery help make even a small room feel very spacious. Here an interesting use of symmetry (two lamps, two mirrors, two tables on either side of the main sofa) gives this room a formal quality that you can easily soften if you prefer.

▶ A sketchy pen and ink-printed fabric adds elegant pattern to enliven a plain sofa.

BEDROOM

As long as you like muted colour schemes in three or four harmonious shades, there is a Scandinavian bedroom to suit you. If you love glamorous, romantic themes you will certainly find the highly decorative painted wooden freestanding furniture ideal, while modernists can focus on a streamlined metal bedstead.

Minimal clutter is the password for creating this serene and relaxing bedroom style. White walls are *de rigueur* and the bed should be the main feature in the room, with white sheets and preferably European-style square pillows. Flooring is usually wooden, although it can be softened by a large cotton-weave rug, and the only other adornments are two or three items of freestanding storage and perhaps a chair.

▸ **A chambray cushion cover has been simply decorated by sewing a delicately patterned fabric patch on to the front. The crisp white with green and blue foliage finish strikes the perfect delicate note.**

bedroom essentials

✔ freestanding storage, in particular a **whitewashed wardrobe** on legs
✔ low-level bed with wood or **canvas headboard** for modern schemes or a pine or white-painted wooden bedstead or four-poster for a more traditional style
✔ **leggy bedside tables** with a drawer and perhaps a cupboard
✔ **bedside lamps** and over-bed directional reading spotlights
✔ wooden flooring or white-glossed **painted floorboards** softened with a cotton rug
✔ floaty voile or **muslin curtains** in plain or two-tone checks, teamed with a wooden venetian blind or painted shutters
✔ **ornate mirror** with a white-painted or gilded frame
✔ **crystal pendant** or wall lights

▸ **For colour and a suggestion of country charm, a wooden wardrobe has been painted and the doors stencilled with a classic Scandinavian motif. Although the wardrobe is coloured, the shades – frosty fir, duck-egg blue, ivory and softest cherry red – are all still fairly subdued.**

◀ **A** white scroll-design chandelier with crystal drops adds shimmering light and a romantic note. If you cannot find a white one, revamp a cheap black pendant chandelier with spray paint, which can be lightly rubbed over with a silver wax stick for extra glisten.

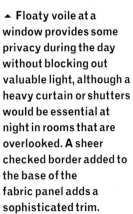

▲ Floaty voile at a window provides some privacy during the day without blocking out valuable light, although a heavy curtain or shutters would be essential at night in rooms that are overlooked. A sheer checked border added to the base of the fabric panel adds a sophisticated trim.

◀ Blue and white checks give this bedroom a fresh and informal look, making it an ideal choice for the average suburban home. The quilted bedspread adds subtle texture and the bedside table and occasional chair are totally authentic to the look.

BATHROOM

As originators of the sauna, Scandinavians naturally love steam-cleaning and ultra-hygienic bathrooms. They prefer streamlined schemes that focus on natural wood and easy-clean ceramic finishes, with hardly any obvious colour.

Many Scandinavians would quite happily sacrifice a bath for a large powerful shower as they see it as an infinitely more hygienic way to get clean than sitting in a tub of bath water. In fact, it is not unusual for Scandinavians – especially the Swedes – to make space for a personal sauna in their own home, too. Clean, uncluttered spaces with lots of sensible storage are the ultimate aim. A combination of fitted and freestanding storage units helps keep the room tidy, while mirrors and halogen spotlights ensure that it is bright. For a more modern look, choose streamlined sanitary ware, such as a back-to-wall suite, with built-in furniture. Tiled walls and floors, preferably in all-white, are the most authentic choice.

bathroom **essentials**

✔ **freestanding storage units**, including a fitted cupboard around the sink (often on legs)
✔ wooden **tongue-and-groove bath panel** with grooves running horizontally sauna style
✔ at least one **large mirror**
✔ halogen recessed **spotlighting** in the ceiling
✔ **white tiles** on walls and floors

▾ **Plant textures, such as wicker and rattan, emphasize the fresh back-to-nature feel of Scandinavian style. A laundry bin complete with sponge seat makes a stylish addition to this type of bathroom.**

▸ **This eye-catching, freestanding basin unit combines the rustic natural pine of country Scandinavian style with sleek, chic, shiny chrome, more commonly associated with high-tech looks, for a distinctively quirky finish that would add character to any bathroom. The slatted wooden shelves offer additional close-to-hand storage, and could be perfectly echoed with a slatted wooden bath mat.**

◀ Monobloc taps with a single control and spout for hot and cold water are by far the most common option for both Scandinavian kitchens and bathrooms. They can't be fitted to an existing two-tap sink but do consider this option when you come to upgrade a suite.

▼ With its back-to-wall toilet, semi-recessed basin and sleek enclosed storage, this sophisticated bathroom fulfils the essential streamlined look of Scandinavian style. The pale blue-grey walls are cool yet fresh and are prevented from looking too cold by being teamed with warm, pale beech wooden furniture and bath panel. The over-bath shower is not totally authentic as most Scandinavians prefer to fit a stand-alone shower, but this bathroom does prove how easily you can adapt all the key ingredients to suit your lifestyle wherever you live.

ETHNIC STYLE 8

8 ETHNIC STYLE

Lavishly exotic in terms of colour and ornamentation, the ethnic look is just about as far as you can get from minimalist style and so is perfect for those with a passion for life who want their home to reflect their sense of adventure.

Based on sun-drenched shades and rich jewel tones, ethnic schemes create a warm and cosy atmosphere, providing a surprisingly lived-in feel that is ideal for a laid-back family home. Ethnic style covers an increasingly wide variety of interior choices from different parts of the world but has come to be synonymous mainly with Moroccan and Indian interiors. These two décor styles focus on the same key features, using sumptuous silks, beading, brass and tin accessories, silk rugs against hard flooring and solid dark wood furniture such as iroko for richly layered looks. Of the two schemes, Moroccan style has a more limited colour palette and tends to inject colour into rooms in the form of soft furnishings and accessories against all-white or plaster pink walls, making it the better option for those who want to dabble rather than commit to all-out colour. It is also the better choice for rooms that suffer from lack of light. Indian style, on the other hand, deliberately clashes colours from opposite sides of the colour spectrum, such as fuchsia pink and cobalt blue – not only on furniture but on walls and even ceilings, too. Not for the fainthearted, this deliciously exuberant décor style will transform the blandest house on even the tightest of budgets.

◄ Softly colourwashed plaster pink walls create a warming atmosphere in this exotic living room and make the perfect backdrop to richly patterned upholstery and cushions on the dark wooden bench seating. The brass-topped tables are authentically Moroccan, as is the stunning ceramic urn, while a palm adds an exotic touch.

is this **the right look** for me?

Ethnic style is ideal for you if you:

✔ love to express your **individuality**

✔ are a secret hoarder of an **eclectic** range of possessions

✔ like the idea of a **glamorous** but lived-in scheme

✔ are inspired by **different cultures** when on holiday

✔ dream of **living abroad** somewhere exotic

✔ want to experiment with **strong colours** to create moods in each room

Avoid if any of the following is true:

✗ I like a strong **sense of order**

✗ I prefer **coordinated** schemes

✗ I am a little **scared of mixing** a wide variety of colours

✗ I need a **calming**, relaxing home environment

✗ I hate being a **slave** to modern fashion

key characteristics

- **Vibrant colour schemes featuring jewel shades offset against terracotta and brilliant white.**

- **Boldly coloured fabrics such as silks and muslins used lavishly – for example draped above a bed as a canopy.**

- **Brassware, from side tables to lanterns with hole-punched patterns.**

- **Rusted wrought-iron scrollwork screens or window shutters.**

- **Ornate dark wood fretwork, perhaps featured on a bedhead.**

- **Cool tiled floors or natural floor-coverings such as seagrass.**

- **Silk rugs for floors and even wall hangings for an opulent focal point for plain walls.**

- **Glass star-shaped ceiling lights and candles.**

▲ A dramatic four-poster bed complete with sumptuous fabric canopy is the epitome of the romantic ethnic bedroom. Pale gold walls and carpeting prevent the authentic wooden furniture looking too dominant, proving that rich furnishings and dark woods need not make a room feel claustrophobic or smaller than it really is.

◄ If you prefer to hint at ethnic style rather than go all out for a themed room, use subtle details rather than dramatic statements. These bathroom walls are subtly decorated with a gold paisley wall stamp, while a simple silk draped curtain panel and pared-back use of *tikka masala* red paint to dado level create a toned down look.

COLOUR

Hot and earthy are two good words to describe the ethnic colour palette – a smouldering clash of vivid shades that excite the senses and give any room distinctive impact. Moroccan style is slightly more sophisticated, being less broad in its colour choices and often featuring large areas of pure white to avoid an overwhelming onslaught of colour. Indian style, on the other hand, is an adventure in high contrast shades, with more not less being the driving force, and here white is hardly used at all.

moroccan style

As befits its North African origins, the rich and warming Moroccan room scheme features burnt desert tones of ochre, sand and terracotta on floors and pillars, set against the stark contrast of dazzling white walls. Jewel-inspired shades such as amber, agate, turquoise, emerald and sapphire are then mixed in, often in the form of mosaics on walls, pillars and even tabletops, to add vibrancy. Richer reds, burgundies and even navy blue may also be introduced with Persian rugs.

• Think **spices** and **jewels**

TONES LIKE:

	white		**turquoise**
	saffron		**emerald**
	cinnamon		**sapphire**
	rust		blue

TEAM WITH:

*   **terracotta-tiled floors**
*   **rusted metal scrollwork accessories**
*   **painted glass and star-shaped lanterns –
    particularly in beaten tin or goatskin
    stretched over wrought-iron light frames
    and decorated with henna motifs**
*   **mosaic tabletops**
*   **fretwork window shutters**

colour tips

Not only do the two ethnic looks featured here focus on quite different palettes of colour, they also use the colours in a very different way.

- **Moroccan style**, which is the more sophisticated of the two, tends to use brilliant white quite heavily on walls, then layer on lots of earthy tones and finally complete each room with just a few accessories in the bolder jewel shades, such as sapphire and emerald, for dramatic contrast. This makes it the more simple to put together and also means it is well suited to homes where lack of light is an issue.
- **Indian style** on the other hand rarely uses white or neutral shades, tending to mix clashing shades on every available surface. It takes more skill to put together but the result has the biggest 'wow' factor of any décor style. To create Indian style successfully, use just three of the hot shades plus gold and silver. That is plenty of adventure for any beginner unless you are very confident with colour. Use a patterned sari fabric you like as inspiration for the rest of your scheme; this will make choosing the perfect colour combination stress free.

indian style

Imagine an Indian marketplace filled with women in exotic yet clashing saris and you have the essence of this exuberant, lustrous colour palette. The beauty of the interior style is that you can opt for a shockingly high-contrast combination of shades, such as hot pink with bold blue, or tone the look down by mixing saffron with tikka and vermilion, for example, for a warm yet still intoxicating look.

- Think **hot exotic, sari** shades

TONES LIKE:

- gold
- turmeric
- tikka red/ brown
- hot pink
- amethyst
- vermilion
- cobalt blue
- lime green
- peacock

TEAM WITH:

- silk bed canopies and layered muslin curtains
- a multitude of rugs overlapping criss-cross on floors
- dark wood furniture
- gold or brass accessories – from tables to lanterns
- sari panels draped on walls or at windows

WALLS

Variety is the spice of life when it comes to choosing how to decorate your walls for ethnic style. Gilded stamped motifs add glitter and sparkle to fit with Indian themes, while rough plaster and tiled finishes, including mosaic, suit the earthy nature of Moroccan style.

Brilliant white walls are the best and most authentic backdrop for Moroccan settings and allow you to use even small helpings of the jewel toned colour palette on seating, curtaining and so on to create an exotic effect. Interestingly, matt finishes are far more common not only on walls but on every surface – the only exception being the use of mosaics on columns and small panels of wall, which give off the dull sheen of ceramic tiles. Indian style takes the directly opposite view turning up the volume on both colour intensity and high sheen on walls. Dramatic highlights of gold and silver are not uncommon on decorative panelling, fretwork or stamped motifs, and of course saris and decorative panels of fabric swathed on poles add to the opulent effect. Your choice of paint finish also depends on which region you take for inspiration. Indian style looks best teamed with higher-sheen finishes such as satin woodwork and silk paints. You could even add metallic finishes on woodwork to create yet more sparkle.

◄ **The paisley motif, so common on Indian saris, makes a stylish stamped effect on plain painted walls. The look can be quickly achieved using gold or silver paint and a paisley design rubber stamp. Do not worry** about measuring accurately between stamps, just use your eye to get a random but fairly evenly spaced look.

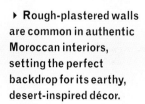

▶ **Rough-plastered walls are common in authentic Moroccan interiors, setting the perfect backdrop for its earthy, desert-inspired décor.**

◂ Moroccan walls feature little except carefully considered embellishments such as dramatic dark wood mirrors similar to the one shown. Here, it is simply propped against a wall although it could look fantastic hung above a mantelpiece or as an eye-catching accessory in an entrance hall.

◂ This two-tone diamond tiled pattern is not authentic but creates a strongly Moroccan feel by mixing matt and shiny tiles in two stunning Moroccan shades. The small mosaic border around the top of the bath panel adds a contemporary touch, yet hints at the ethnic origins of mosaic wall style.

▴ For maximum impact use the full force of the ethnic palette by coating your walls in vibrant colours. Painting all four walls in just one shade gives a pared-back version, but layering several shades will create the true eclectic ethnic look. Let your imagination flow.

F LOORS

The hot and dusty conditions typical of India and Morocco mean that practical, low-maintenance flooring, which is cooling to the touch, is the essential choice. Tiled floors are simple to brush clean or wipe, which is why they are so often used in the ethnic home.

Stone and particularly terracotta tiles add richness yet are relatively informal, which is why they are commonly used in the average home, while glossy marble is more often found in top-class hotels. Adding scatter rugs throughout allows you to give rooms a layer of softness and can be used in one of two ways. For grand, opulent rooms one large rug positioned centrally is ideal, while for more laid-back family rooms a selection of three or more smaller rugs positioned slightly overlapping one another in haphazard, perhaps

criss-cross pattern is far more in keeping. If you must have carpet, look for rich paisley motifs or plain or ribbed neutral tones so you are at least adhering to the colour palettes on pages 164–5.

Natural fibre floorings can also be used to mimic authentic rush matting. Seagrass is the smoothest underfoot. Finally, if you really want to give your imagination free rein, consider creating a patterned mosaic floor in a bathroom or hallway for the ultimate eye-catching choice.

◀ **Seagrass or sisal natural fibre flooring is not strictly authentic but suits the earthy back-to-nature look of Moroccan rooms, although it is not opulent enough for an Indian theme. Look for large basket-weave designs like the one shown for a chunky, rustic look and a durable finish underfoot, ideal for rugs in hallways in particular.**

▶ **Bold geometric-patterned rugs fit the ethnic look if you want to add a modern twist. For true authenticity, though, silk or Persian-style ornamental rugs laid with criss-crossing overlapping edges are ideal, and they make great wall hangings, too.**

▾ Bold Moroccan star motifs on hand-painted tiles add drama underfoot but are best confined to smaller rooms to avoid an overwhelming end result.

▴ Terracotta tiles interspersed with small inset tiles and laid slightly offset give a quirky finish that hints at ethnic origins. Here a cotton dhurrie rug with tasselled edges adds softness for bare feet and for warmth as you step out of a hot bath.

◂ This rich golden-coloured carpet echoes the look of sand, making it a good option in homes where comfort is of prime importance. Rougher-cut piles such as a twist will suit the scheme best, but although plain is perfect, many manufacturers have taken inspiration from Moroccan imagery to incorporate stylish motifs in a regular pattern that can work well, too.

FABRICS

At their most extreme, ethnic-themed fabrics are the loudest in pattern, the brightest in colour and the most heavily embroidered of any décor style, so even used in small doses they can lend an instant air of exoticism to almost any home.

Bold, vibrant and bejewelled, ethnic fabrics used in the form of just a few accessories – such as cushions or curtains – can introduce a sense of ethnic style without necessitating a whole new scheme. Use the colour palette as a guide and remember that your choice of texture depends on which country you want to emulate most: silks, organzas and open-weave muslins suit the Indian theme, while heavy velvets add a Moroccan feel. Have fun experimenting with mixing richly patterned fabrics with plains to achieve a

balance that suits your own taste. Indian fabrics tend to feature paisley motifs, gold and silver embroidery, lots of hand-embroidered beading and even tiny mirrors hand-stitched in place for added sparkle. Use traditional Indian imagery of temples, elephants and gods if you prefer a more patterned end result. Moroccan fabrics generally rely on texture and block-printed motifs for interest and have a richer yet more subdued look. Geometric Moroccan star motifs work brilliantly used on selective soft furnishings.

‹ Hand embroidered with paisley motifs, these hot pink and purple cushions echo an Indian flavour without being too ornate.

› Add pattern and drama with elephant and temple motifs or simple gold prints on rich coloured backgrounds – ideal for upholstery.

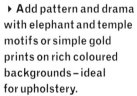

‹ A relatively subdued choice of colours in burnt orange, gold, cream and dark green gives a sophisticated twist on ethnic style, and prevents a busy pattern being too overwhelming.

KITCHEN

Experimentation is the key to creating an ethnic-style kitchen. There isn't one stereotypical look so the only limit is your imagination. Use hot tropical shades for cupboards or add accessories to a simple wooden kitchen for a subtle effect. Whatever your budget it's easy to echo the mood.

The kitchen in the average Moroccan and Indian home is basic by European or American standards, with an open wood-burning oven just as likely to appear as a modern gas or electric appliance. But the fact that there are no definitive guidelines as to how to recreate the look actually frees you to play with colour and accessories rather than opting for a radical overhaul – a big bonus for those on a budget. Using dark wood units is one good starting point as it echoes the use of iroko and dark teak in other rooms in the ethnic home. However, mid-toned rustic wood finishes can easily be given an ethnic twist with the addition of saffron walls and traditional ethnic accessories, including brass and tin cookware, wooden gourds and hand-painted tiles. Just remember that the more informal and haphazard the look the better, as casual clutter is key.

kitchen essentials

- ✔ **dark wood** or marble work-tops
- ✔ stone flooring, especially **terracotta**
- ✔ **mosaic** splashback
- ✔ **freestanding units** rather than a fitted look
- ✔ **hand-painted** ceramic tiles in mix-and-match designs

▲ **This modern interpretation of Moroccan style shows how you can create an ethnic feel in your kitchen/diner without succumbing to clutter. Handmade brushed-iron seating, a mosaic-tiled tabletop, hand-woven plates and a coloured glass star lantern are all you need to echo authentic furnishings against bold walls.**

▸ **While it might be authentic to sit on floor cushions to eat a Moroccan meal, an ornately carved dark wood dining table and chairs offer a practical alternative that is still in keeping with the whole theme.**

◄ Here a fairly ordinary mid-toned wood kitchen is transformed with saffron-coloured walls, hand-painted tiles and unique ethnic accessories, such as wooden gourds hung from shelves. These can add an exotic look without huge Investment or long-term commitment to the style. Cosy clutter gives the room a warm and earthy feel but only as long as you select the items for display with great care.

▼ Beaded linen brings an opulent note to your dining table, making it perfect for a sophisticated dinner party. For a really lavish look, mix the colours of table mats and napkins from place to place.

LIVING ROOM

A sense of drama and intimacy is essential in the ethnic living room. In authentic Moroccan schemes, seating is at floor level on piles of sumptuous cushions or mattress-style seat pads covered with opulent but durable fabrics.

In Indian schemes, dark wood and rush seating in the form of ornately carved daybeds and colonial-style armchairs are more usual. These are not really practical options for everyday life, so look for low-level sofas in minimalist designs – with a low back and no arms if possible – but in deep upholstery shades such as wine red, which you can then accessorize with lots of scatter cushions. These should be richly embroidered, beaded or even have tiny mirrors sewn on the front. Dark wood furniture is perfect – a Thakat-style table in deep mahogany with wrought-iron detailing will provide the look you are after and is widely available on the high street and from mail-order suppliers. Moroccan homes also feature mosaic-topped side and coffee tables on narrow, pole-style iron legs or round, beaten-brass side tables.

▶ Our ethnic-style living room features opulent jewel tones on every surface, set against the richness of dark wood furniture. The ornate daybed and vibrant hand-embroidered wall hanging are much more Indian in design, while the coffee table, cabinet and embossed tin mirror would sit equally well in a more subdued Moroccan scheme. The gold paisley motif on the walls is pure Indian style, too, and was applied by hand with a rubber stamp.

◀ A vibrant sari draped at a window is not an authentic window dressing but it is a brilliantly easy way to interpret ethnic style. Saris can be bought fairly easily, for example from Indian clothing stores in city centres and are relatively cheap, depending on the amount of embroidery. Simply drape your sari over a gold or wrought-iron curtain pole, but remember that you will need to add a blind for privacy at night.

▲ This handmade leather pouffe is actually from Egypt but is representative of the low-level seating to be found across the whole of North Africa. It is also ideal as a footstool.

living room essentials

- ✔ silk or vibrant cotton **floor cushions**
- ✔ **silk rugs**
- ✔ wrought-iron, beaten animal hide or glass and **silver lanterns** for Moroccan style
- ✔ brass lanterns and **wall sconces** for Indian style
- ✔ **wall hangings**
- ✔ **dark wood** coffee table

▸ **These colourful ribbed glass lanterns with aged brass fittings are authentic Indian lighting. Although they hold candles, it is possible to buy electric versions that mimic the effect in a more practical way.**

▾ **The classic hexagon design and compact size of this painted wooden and iron Moroccan tea table make it a wonderful choice for a sofa end or corner table. The Moroccan tea glasses on top draw attention to its original function.**

BEDROOM

You can almost smell the incense when you walk into a dramatic ethnic-inspired bedroom, for the rich colour scheme, heavy fabrics, wall hangings and dramatic bed all evoke a feeling of intense exoticism. Great for boudoirs, but not for shy retiring types.

Think of a harem theme to set your imagination loose when designing this room setting, then consider ways to replace or revamp your boring divan. Ethnic bedrooms always have a dramatic bed as the main focal point of the room so consider investing in a carved wooden four-poster for an exotic boudoir feel. Ornately carved headboards in dark wood, such as iroko, create a distinctly Moroccan flavour – but look out for designs that extend at least 1m (3ft) above your divan to give the bed real dominance. For a more Indian flavour, drape heavy swathes of fabric above the bedhead to create a cocoon around your pillows, or suspend a mosquito net from a hooped hanging frame centred above the bed to mimic colonial style. Carved wooden bedside tables make ideal accompaniments, as does a large carved chest as a blanket box.

▾ **No exotic bedroom would be complete without the romantic flickering of candlelight to set the mood. Choose brass lanterns or vibrantly coloured candles in gilded glass holders for a safe yet opulent look and remember never to leave lit candles unattended.**

▸ **Silk or satin beaded bolster cushions are ideal for adding a luxurious touch to a bed for a hint of ethnic style. They would work equally well piled up at either end of a plain sofa.**

bedroom essentials

✔ **low-level** bed
✔ **draped canopy** or mosquito net or ornately carved wooden headboard
✔ **coloured glass** ceiling light or punched-metal lantern
✔ candelabra **wall sconces**
✔ **ornately carved** dark wood bedside tables

▸ **A wooden fretwork folding screen, like this one made from sheeshram wood with a dark mahogany stain, is a wonderfully exotic addition to a bedroom and is great for hiding clutter that threatens to overwhelm the room.**

Inspired by the hot pinks and cobalt blues of the Indian colour palette, this scheme proves that you can use the essentials of ethnic style to create a similar but more pared-back look suitable for the average home. A sari hung from a curtain pole adds dramatic focus behind the bed and is pulled into gathers in the front by threading it through Indian bangles. Hand stencils used for henna printing at weddings are framed to make exotic artwork for the walls and a standard duvet cover is dyed hot pink and decorated with a panel of organza and embroidered Indian silk to complete the effect.

◀ This traditional fretwork nickel-plated lantern is a replica of those found in Moroccan mosques and casts a beautiful kaleidoscope of light around your room, although for maximum impact its design is best suited to those with higher ceilings.

BATHROOM

Let your imagination run wild in this room to create an exotic sanctuary in which to bathe while you dream of being in sunnier climes. Rough-plastered walls teamed with tiles on floors, walls and shower enclosures are the most authentic starting point … then pile on the colour.

The need to keep fresh and cool underpins the style of ethnic bathrooms, so tiles cover almost every surface and should form the basis for your look. Modern Moroccan looks are most accessible, with their subdued limestone or marble tiling, but why not experiment with bright mosaic flooring or wall tiles in aqua, blue, white and burnt sand hues. A large walk-in shower fits the theme more than a bath, so you might consider swapping your standard bathroom for an exotic wet room, tiled from floor to ceiling, with a dramatic large rose shower head simply fixed to one wall, so that the shower cubicle and room are effectively one and the same. Alternatively, you could take inspiration from colonial days and opt for a freestanding roll-top bath instead. Add shutters or fretwork screening to your windows for privacy. Decorate the room with brass or tin punched mirrors and lanterns and handmade polished ironwork accessories such as a freestanding towel rail.

bathroom essentials

✔ **terracotta**-tiled floors
✔ **fretwork** window shutters
✔ **mosaic tiles** on walls, floors or even a work-top for an inset basin
✔ **soft lighting** for a moody atmosphere
✔ wrought-iron or **aged brassware** towel rails, robe hooks, and so on

▲ **This authentic Moroccan basin features a rough plaster pedestal effect and an inset, glazed ceramic bowl with typical print design.**

▸ **Hole-punched or embossed tin is commonly used in Moroccan and Indian schemes in the form of lanterns but also as a sheet covering for furniture and mirrors or picture frames, such as the one shown here. You can create a similar effect with tin sheeting from a metal suppliers – punched with holes using a bradawl.**

▲ With their patterned perforations these neat shutters, made from **MDF**, fake an ethnic look adding privacy without blocking out the light.

◄ For pure ethnic fantasy, this bathroom has been given a dramatic look with cobalt-blue walls, a simple hand-painted mosaic-design border on the walls and an enticing, if somewhat frivolous, mosquito net set above a freestanding roll-top bath. The tiled floor and window shutters are perhaps the most authentic features of the room, but though the other elements would never be found in Indian or Moroccan homes, there is no denying the influence.

AMERICAN COUNTRY STYLE 9

9 AMERICAN COUNTRY STYLE

Homespun touches, such as patchwork quilts and hand-stitched sampler pictures, used in small doses plus sleek hand-carved furniture in natural woods capture the essential character of American country style. This simplistic yet charming décor is both practical and cosy, making it ideal for any family home.

▲ With its bold red, white and blue colour scheme and distressed paint-effect tongue-and-groove panelling, this bathroom shows off the essentials of New England design with a definite rustic twist. The charming patchwork pictures add a homespun feel and would fit just as comfortably in a simple cream and wood Shaker scheme.

American country style has two strands: the Shaker style and its modern interpretation, known as New England style. Both use the same key elements to create homely yet highly practical interiors. Shaker style takes its name from the Shakers, a religious community formed in the mid-18th century as an offshoot of the Quakers, which established itself in America. The Shakers lived and worked together in self-sufficient communities. They built their own homes and crafted high-quality furniture, using the motto 'beauty in utility' as their guiding principle. Solid wooden furniture, hand-carved in maple and cherry and following the same designs is still made today and its stylish simplicity is perfect for a timeless, classic look. The Shaker kitchen in particular has inspired any number of designs currently available on the high street. Lovers of country style focus on the Shaker use of ginghams, hand-embroidered pictures, quilts and wrought-iron accessories for a pretty twist on the theme. Hand and heart motifs are also integral, together with wooden carved birds and bird houses, but the look can be interpreted in a modern pared-back way, too. New England style is a bolder, more up-to-date version of the same basic look. It features the streamlined Shaker furniture designs and the wooden flooring and tongue-and-groove wall panelling, but opts for more intense tones of the colour palette (especially red, white and blue) to give a vibrant, crisp and distinctly all-American look.

◄ American country style is given a modern feel here with a rattan rather than a wooden bedstead, and a boldly geometric bedspread cover instead of the more traditional patchwork quilt. This shows the adaptability of this design style to both new-built and period homes.

key characteristics

- **Natural wood flooring, decorated with plain or two-tone checked weave rugs.**

- **Solid wooden furniture in pared-back unfussy designs in pale cherry or maple, or painted in muted matt colours such as sage, duck-egg blue, cream or taupe.**

- **White-painted walls or tongue-and-groove shiplap-style panelling.**

- **Picture rail-height peg rails running around a room for hanging everything from utensils and laundry bags to shelving units, mirrors and even chairs so as to keep floor space clutter free for cleaning.**

- **Gingham or checked materials used in subdued amounts for subtle interest.**

- **Cross-stitch hand-embroidery.**

- **Heart and hand motifs and bird-box or carved wooden bird accessories in distressed paint finishes for an aged effect.**

- **Wrought-iron accessories – particularly in the bathroom.**

◄ Hand-crafted furniture creates an authentically pared-back yet tranquil traditional Shaker scheme based on 18th-century designs. The delightfully elegant oval-lidded coffee table-cum-storage box is based on a Shaker original. All the furniture displays the traditional fabric lattice-woven seating and finial-topped posts.

is this **the right look** for me?

American country style is ideal for you if you:
- ✔ need a **practical scheme** but nothing stark or minimalist
- ✔ want a **cosy family** home
- ✔ prefer **subtle detail** to stand-alone, eye-catching furniture
- ✔ need lots of cleverly designed **storage**

Avoid if any of the following is true:
- ✗ I love **lots of colour** and pattern
- ✗ I like **high-tech appliances** on open view
- ✗ I prefer **high-fashion looks** at low cost for frequent updates
- ✗ I get easily bored with **one type** of scheme

COLOUR

Taking its inspiration from the natural world, the traditional Shaker palette is made up primarily of creams and greens, with reds and blues introduced in the form of accessories such as gingham and patchwork, making it perfect for soft, tranquil colour schemes. The New England palette, which is the modern interpretation of the look, is far more bold and lively, focusing instead on vibrant red and blue tones against predominantly white or off-white walls for a more invigorating room scheme but the same clutter-free finish.

traditional shaker style

The vast majority of the traditional range of shades have a soft, smudgy, earthy undertone, due in part to the fact that original Shaker paints were made with pigments taken from clays and plants with added milk or casein, which gives them this hazy, matt charm. Except for the accent shades of red, navy and teal blue, the colours blend to create a subtle, harmonious scheme, perfect when used on walls for giving a light, airy, open feel to a room.

• Think **farmyard** and **woodland-inspired** shades

TONES LIKE:

		Accent shades:
cream		
buttermilk		**Indian red**
mushroom		**scarlet**
lichen		**navy**
moss		
dark duck-egg blue		
teal		
forest green		

TEAM WITH:

• **mid-toned wooden furniture and flooring**
• **wooden knob handles on furniture**
• **wrought-iron accessories**
• **punched-tin lanterns**
• **bird-boxes**
• **hand-sewn cross-stitched bedlinens**

colour tips

Can't decide which of the two American country looks to opt for? Then think about your home and lifestyle to make the most practical choice. **Traditional Shaker style**, with its creamy yet sludgy colour palette, has a sophisticated yet period feel, which works best in older properties where it looks most authentic. Pale furnishings also mean that unless you have a neat and orderly family, keeping it looking spartan, fresh and clean may be a battle too big to win. However, it is ideal for clutter-hating couples who like the idea of a country look but without all the frills.

The more contemporary and high-contrast colours of **New England style** are equally fresh but combine to create more invigorating décor, which works well in both light and less well-lit rooms, and both old and new properties. The bold colour schemes also help detract the eye from a little clutter and the modern incorporation of denim and leather upholstery makes the style family-friendly, too.

new england style

For a modern twist, New England-style rooms take the accent colours of the Shaker palette and make them the main colours in the scheme, focusing on bold shades of red, white and blue for a real American feel. In essence, the New England style is about reinterpreting the original Shaker look, taking colours and furnishings several stages further. So, for example, you will find that crisp bold checks are far more common than pretty ginghams.

• Think **vivid primary** shades

TONES LIKE:

white		chestnut
cream		teal
beige		navy blue
scarlet		

TEAM WITH:

- **leather and denim upholstery**
- **crisp bold checks**
- **wooden flooring**
- **silver or painted accessories**

WALLS

Rustic simplicity is the watchword when choosing American country-style walls. The essential thing to remember is that the walls should be kept as plain as possible to act merely as a backdrop for the limited colour palette and the pared-back furniture that exemplify this décor.

Whitewashed walls in a matt-finish paint are the most common option used throughout the American country home, but textured finishes such as rough plaster and tongue-and-groove panelling are suitably rustic, yet pared-back too, as long as you decorate them only in subdued nature-inspired shades to avoid turning them into focal points.

No self-respecting American country scheme would be complete without at least one peg rail. If you choose not to run the rail right around your room, fixing it to just one focal wall will add a note of authenticity, as well as providing you with useful storage. It is ideal in a cramped guest room where a wardrobe would take up too much valuable space. Copies of peg rails are widely available, but you could also make your own with smooth-finished pine battening and tiny drawer knobs screwed in at regular intervals. Hang spare chairs from it in a kitchen when your dining area is not in use. Other decorative features, such as patchwork samplers, also look cute in limited doses.

▲ The Shakers created purpose-made shelves, mirrors and even cupboards with leather hoop fixings or hanging holes carved into the wood itself. This meant that these moderate weight items could be wall hung from a peg rail and moved around at will from room to room for the ultimate in flexibility and practicality. Modern versions are still made by the Shaker community today.

◀ **Hand-stitched patchwork samplers** in traditional red, white and blue and with hand or heart motifs make charming and authentic wall hangings. Attach your own tab-top heading and hang from dowelling fixed straight and level to your wall.

▶ **Rough-textured wooden panelling** gives instant rustic charm to a room and takes on a Shaker look when painted, as here, in a sludgy moss green. This is simply rough-hewn boarding, with gaps in between, fixed directly to the wall, giving a much more homespun finish than tongue and groove. Adding battening on top to create rectangular panels shows attention to detail and completes the look.

◀ **Tiles** were not used in original Shaker homes, but nowadays it would be impractical not to use them as splashbacks. Look for handmade ivory or white tiles to suit the clean, simple rustic theme of traditionally inspired rooms, or consider using gingham-check or heart-motif tiles in small doses.

▶ **Plain matt whitewashed walls** with a chalky texture are the first choice for authentic schemes, and soft white is far preferable to modern synthetic 'brilliant' whites, which look far too harsh. Perfect for giving a spacious feel, white walls throughout a home create flow from room to room and work well with both rustic and more sophisticated looks.

FLOORS

Natural materials are the only choice for flooring in an interior décor style that relies on inspiration, and indeed product-sourcing, from the natural world. However, this does not mean that your schemes have to look hard and unenticing.

Real wood floorboards are without doubt the most authentic choice for this homely style. They exemplify the reliance of the use of materials taken directly from nature, and add a warm tone, too. Plus wood combines both the rustic spirit and a note of sophistication to suit both Shaker and New England looks. Adding woven cotton rugs helps break up large expanses of wooden floor and makes this choice more accessible for the family home, too. All natural fibres such as coir, seagrass and sisal will sit comfortably

with American country décor. Flagstone flooring is another option, perfect for echoing the farmhouse feel in a kitchen or hallway. Invest in the real thing to maximize the impact and charm of colour differentiation from tile to tile for a less regular and manufactured look. Finally, avoid manmade materials such as vinyl and carpet if you want to be true to Shaker style, although you can get away with using these flooring alternatives in the modern New England-inspired schemes.

◀ **Real wood flooring is totally in keeping with the all-natural look of the Shaker-style home, but go for cherry or maple effects to coordinate with furniture or stain existing floorboards a darker shade to give a naturally aged effect.**

◄ **Natural-textured carpeting or flooring is not authentic for traditional Shaker style but suits the more cosy New England look well. Choose a cross-hatch weave for a more rustic finish.**

◄ Rugs are essential for softening the predominantly hard wood flooring. Bold checked cotton-weave rugs are ideal, or coir style edged with a gingham border is another attractive and more subtle alternative that will withstand lots of wear and tear.

▲ Flagstones make a wonderful choice for kitchens and hallways, giving the desired practical, nature-inspired look, although quarry tiles would do the job just as well. They should ideally be made from local materials to be in keeping with the materials used when your house was built and the colours of soil in the garden.

FABRICS

Natural-fibre fabrics are essential if you want to be totally authentic, as the Shakers produced their own materials, including wool, cotton and flax. Pattern is kept to a fuss-free minimum with checks and subtle hand-embroidery being the most effective choices to add interest.

Shaker style offers a rather limited choice of material options to the decorator, which can be a positive bonus as once you know what to look for it is hard to make a mistake. The main reason for this was that Shaker homes did not feature upholstered furniture, and windows were decorated with shutters instead of curtaining. Fabric was used primarily for table and bedlinens and small homemade accessories. On the whole, the Shakers worked with plain or plain dyed hand-woven fabrics, which they coloured with natural plant dyes. Subtle checks and ginghams in two or more colours were used for contrast, for example in the form of patchwork quilting, and hand-embroidery was often used to add subtle pattern to bedlinens and even tea towels but only in limited amounts. New England looks offer a much broader fabric range, including durable denims and even leather for upholstery. The New England look also features bigger bolder checked patterns to add a deliberately modern note.

◄ Patchwork remains one of the most popular American handicrafts, revered for its nostalgic quality and the pleasure to be had from creating a work of art. Bedspreads which can be handed down from generation to generation as a treasured heirloom are the most common. Quilting is often a communal activity, and authentic quilts can be worked on by more than one family member at the same time, but no one need know if you prefer to cheat and buy the finished article instead.

◄ Sampler style embroidery in unbleached wools or natural-dyed finishes adds charm to cushion fronts and can also be hung in picture frames to add an informal yet homely flavour to any room.

▶ Decorative cross-stitch used in limited amounts on linens for the bedroom and the kitchen adds a homespun quality to any American country scheme. Look out in particular for heart and hand motifs, which are images still used by the Shaker community today. Usually the fine cross-stitch is limited to just two or three colours in delicate small motifs that add subtle pattern and charm without becoming dominant.

KITCHEN

Shaker style kitchens have been vigorously copied by every high-street kitchen design retailer with diluted versions of this distinctive and pared-back farmhouse look. Simple single panelled doors with knob handles are the essence of this style.

Natural wood units or emulsion painted finishes in the traditional colour palette set the perfect scene. Modern interpretations of the look have introduced slick metal bar handles instead of wooden knobs for a contemporary twist. To be as authentic as possible, a traditional range cooker is a great focal point for this family-orientated scheme, but it is quite feasible to tailor the look with a high-tech stainless steel range to match your silver-handled doors if you choose. In either case, both modern and traditional Shaker kitchens should be well planned and fully fitted to accommodate all your clutter behind closed doors and to keep work-tops as clear as possible – with the exception of the ubiquitous peg rail for a neat row of utensils. For an original touch, you might copy the Shakers and hang kitchen chairs from your peg rail, too, to keep the floor clear when you sweep it clean.

kitchen **essentials**

- ✔ **peg rail**
- ✔ Shaker units with a **simple panel** doors
- ✔ **wooden knob** handles
- ✔ **butler's sink**
- ✔ **Aga** or range cooker
- ✔ **wooden flooring**
- ✔ table and **ladder-back** chairs

▼ **A wide ceramic butler-style sink suits this period look and should be teamed with a real wood or wood-look work-top. Real wood will need regular oiling to maintain its good looks.**

▶ **An enormous solid wooden dresser offers plenty of storage for table linens, cutlery and tableware. Here you can see authentic wooden bowls and hand-carved plates, which can be bought today direct from Shaker communities. If all-wood tableware is too expensive or impractical for your needs, chunky plain white china would create a similarly pared-back display.**

▲ This soft forest green kitchen has a tranquil, nature-inspired look. A maple folding table with authentic Shaker ladder-back chairs takes centre stage while the wood floors, peg rail, utensils and work-top all add warmth for a softly harmonious scheme. Four leaf print images add subtle country charm to the walls.

▶ Yet again the peg rail comes into play, this time in the kitchen, where it can be used to keep a range of utensils out of the way but nearby until they are needed.

LIVING ROOM

Homely and inviting, a New England-style living room is ideal for a family home. With durable carpet or wooden flooring, softened by a cotton-weave rug (often in a checked design), plain white walls and pale maple or cherry furniture, the basics are the same as the traditional Shaker style, but the colour gives it a fresher modern feel.

Mixing a bold red, white and blue palette, creates an instantly contemporary, fresh and invigorating scheme. Where traditional Shaker style uses tiny doses of pretty gingham for a touch of pattern, this modern interpretation splashes on dramatic two-tone checks. Also, while the Shakers' handmade seating consisted of wooden armchairs, rockers or double chair benches with webbed seating, this modern alternative allows you to introduce the home comforts of cosy squashy sofas, and even denim and leather upholstery for contrast.

living room **essentials**

- ✔ **wooden flooring**
- ✔ gingham or **checked accessories** in blue, red and white
- ✔ **checked rug** to soften the floor
- ✔ oval wooden **chest-cum-coffee table** with lid
- ✔ **peg rail** for easy-access storage
- ✔ **denim or leather seating**

▲ **A bold checked cotton-weave rug adds softness and colour to the neutral carpeting and creates a focal point in the centre of the room.**

▼ **While it is by no means an authentic choice, somehow a beaten leather armchair sits perfectly in this more modern scheme. As it is both practical, weathering family use well, and beautiful, it proves that the Shaker motto 'beauty in utility' can be applied to modern home furnishings if they are chosen carefully.**

▲ **Two- or three-tone gingham fabrics are stereotypical of this look and have a charming simplicity. Here patch layers on cushions create interest for a homemade feel, while the heart imagery is consistent with Shaker heritage.**

◀ Removing all signs of clutter is a Shaker virtue, which is why a peg rail makes its appearance in almost every room for easy-to-reach wall-hung storage. Here a simple cloth bag makes the ideal hiding place for children's toys at the end of a day, but it would work just as well for the daily newspaper in an adult home.

▼ This modern living room has all the core elements of American country style, such as the essential peg rail and use of gingham accessories as well as larger-checked patterned curtains, but teams them with contemporary yet cosy furniture, such as a denim-covered sofa and a leather armchair, and a bold red, white and blue colour scheme. The white walls allow for maximum flexibility, so this scheme could be updated in hours with new cushion covers, new curtains and a lick of paint on the peg rail.

BEDROOM

A mid-toned wooden four-poster bed with streamlined posts rather than heavily turned or carved posts is the authentic centrepiece for this style of bedroom, although it is possible to adapt the look to an existing divan, too.

Using a four-poster is a sophisticated twist on the romantic style (although ironically the Shakers themselves believed in celibacy). Rich mid-toned woods such as cherry or maple are the ideal choice for all furniture, but you could opt for painted alternatives instead, based on the American country palette, if painted styles are more to your taste. A strong sense of symmetry is common with two identical bedside tables – either pedestal style or, more commonly, with four legs and a single practical drawer. Your freestanding furniture should provide ample storage and chests of drawers are taller and slimmer than the average.

bedroom **essentials**

✔ solid wood square-topped **leggy bedside table** with single drawer and knob handle
✔ **patchwork quilt**
✔ white bedlinen, perhaps with **cross-stitch border**
✔ large two- or three-door solid wood **wardrobe with drawers** at the base
✔ simple **window shutters** or simple tab-top curtains

▸ **Knitted blankets and throws in unbleached wools or natural dyed finishes provide a cosy touch and are particularly common as an extra layer for a bed.**

▾ **Perfect for creating a truly restful bedroom, the** soft colours of sage and cream team beautifully with a rich wooden four-poster for a sophisticated take on the Shaker look. Lovers of a prettier country style could introduce a charming patchwork quilt, gingham cushions and even embroidered or appliquéd pictures for added charm and yet still keep the authentic look.

▸ **The Shakers' attention to** detail went even as far as creating beautifully hand-crafted storage boxes in this traditional oval-lidded design. They were scaled up or down according to what was to be stored inside and they stack perfectly for a clutter-free scheme.

▾ **The simplicity of** this neat yet practical bedside table is true to all the ideals of Shaker style. The wooden knob handle is essential for a traditional look, while a single drawer and just one shelf provide ample storage and discourage clutter.

BATHROOM

As with all the other rooms, the way you decorate your American country bathroom depends on which aspect of the style you choose to emphasize. Traditional Shaker bathrooms tend to be sparse and practical. A freestanding roll-top bath and plain square-shaped pedestal basin would be most in keeping with the look.

If your bathroom is on the small side or you prefer a more fitted look, using tongue-and-groove panelling on both walls and the fitted bath panel is a clever way to point to rustic influences without sacrificing home comforts. Wooden flooring is almost a given for either look, but remember that wood is not naturally happy in the humid conditions of a bathroom and can warp if splashed repeatedly. Painted floorboards sealed with several good coats of yacht varnish will withstand this best of all. Finally, take your time to select just the right accessories, for these are what will ultimately make or break your scheme. Gingham curtains or shutters are ideal for the window treatment. A freestanding towel rail and wrought-iron accessories such as a curtain pole and toilet-roll holder are also authentic. The Shakers twisted plain ironwork into heart or hand motifs at the ends and it is worth trying to track down something as close as possible for perfect results.

▸ This pretty rustic scheme is given a Shaker flavour with tongue-and-groove panelling and wrought-iron accessories. The rather kitsch four-poster bath surround is a reference to the Shaker four-poster bed, while the gingham curtains soften the look – though no self-respecting Shaker would consider such a frivolous detail.

bathroom **essentials**

- ✔ **tongue-and-groove** panelling on walls and bath panel
- ✔ **wrought-iron accessories** (preferably with a hand or heart motif)
- ✔ **freestanding towel rail** in wood or wrought iron
- ✔ window shutters or **gingham curtains** with simple tie tops
- ✔ **wooden floor**

▸ **Designed to hang from the standard peg rail which ran around every room in the Shaker home, this traditional mirror is a neat and flexible choice that can be moved to wherever it is needed.**

▸ **Wrought-iron hand-crafted towel rails, hooks and even toilet roll holders are now available from modern generations of the Shaker community. Look for those that feature a heart or hand motif like the ones shown.**

◂ Heart shaped pomanders stuffed with herbs or lavender add a charming feature simply hung over a door handle. Made from hand-quilted fabric, this design has a real homespun feel.

◂ Doubling as seating and a laundry bin, this wonderfully crafted storage drum is an authentic Shaker design made from birch-faced ply. It adds a charming detail to a bedroom or bathroom, but would equally provide storage for children's toys.

COASTAL STYLE 10

COASTAL
STYLE

Crisp colours and an endless choice of furniture and accessories make coastal style one of the easiest and most enjoyable looks to put together. Take your inspiration from a postcard or a real-life beach for a room that will set a holiday mood all year round. Who cares if you live miles from the sea?

Inspired by lapping water, sandy beaches and the intriguing textures of bleached driftwood, coastal style has widespread appeal and a highly romanticized image. It can take many forms, depending on the shoreline you use as your inspiration – from nautical navy and white schemes, through seaside-inspired primary shades for a family-friendly home, to the most modern take, based on azure, sky blue and the colours

of sand and pebbles. It is a wonderful scheme to put together because, as one of the most popular styles, it is easy to find accessories and furnishings to suit and immense fun to visit the seaside itself for bright ideas and local finds. Although there are key elements, the look is constantly evolving, so there is something to suit all tastes, and you don't even need to live near water to enjoy the end results.

◄ **Vibrantly painted beach huts were the inspiration behind this bold living room scheme. The bright shades avoid being overwhelming by having the pattern limited to just a few stripy cushions and works of art on the walls, while natural flooring and mid-toned furniture add a sleek finish.**

is this **the right look** for me?

Coastal style is ideal for you if you:

✔ would love to **capture holiday memories** at home

✔ find constant decorating inspiration in the **natural world**

✔ are a **fan of junk-shop bargains** and salvage-yard hunting

✔ like the **basic mood of country style** but without all that pattern

Avoid if any of the following is true:

✗ I live in an **urban apartment**

✗ I hate the idea of rooms **looking other than pristine**

✗ I find **nautical or seaside** imagery too twee

✗ **Blue and white** colour schemes bore me

▲ Fresh blue and white in the bathroom conjure up images of the sea and sky, although the only obvious references to a nautical style are the shell pictures and a sailing boat on the shelf. Subtlety is the key to making this look a success.

◀ Crisp blue Shaker-style units add a breezy seaside feel to this kitchen and are perfectly complemented by wooden flooring, stained with a blue woodwash, and tongue-and-groove panelling on the walls for a rustic feel. Open shelving allows plenty of display space.

key characteristics

● Wood or whitewashed floorboards or neutral-toned textured carpets.

● Tongue-and-groove walls for a textured look inspired by ship's panelling.

● Window shutters or floaty drapes for unfussy, rustic-style windows. Go for rough linens, hessians, cotton muslins and slubby textured cottons.

● Pebbles, driftwood and lanterns used as accessories to add a sense of the outdoors. Seaside scavenging for driftwood can lead to wonderful finds, but bear in mind that removing cobbles from a beach is now illegal in some countries, so buy bags of pebbles from a **DIY** store or garden centre instead.

● Bleached-wood or lime-washed furniture creates a sun-drenched, naturally aged feel – anything new will look wrong in this informal, eclectic scheme.

● Primaries and crisp blue and white are two key colour scheme options. Your choice will depend on whether you want to create a bold, seaside feel or a more muted beach theme. Marine shades of aqua and turquoise are also good for a more contemporary look.

COLOUR

As you would expect, coastal style takes its inspiration for colours of walls, fabrics and furniture directly from seascapes and so focuses almost exclusively on blues, greens and neutral tones in varying intensities and shades. However, this palette can be subdivided further, depending on whether you prefer the more traditional look or like to experiment with bolder, more contemporary shades.

traditional coastal style

Classic nautical room schemes take their inspiration from traditional seaside towns and yachting harbours, with dramatic contrasts of navy and white as the key. Accent shades can be used to add layers of interest, but still in a fairly limited range of colours. Picture in your mind a cheerful row of beach huts along a coastline for the perfect primary shades to choose from for accessories to create a bolder, more contemporary feel if that appeals.

• Think **monotone blue and white** schemes, plus **beach-hut brights**

TONES LIKE:

	sail white		sky blue
	sand		denim blue
	sunflower		French navy
	yellow		scarlet

TEAM WITH:

* **sophisticated classic looks or jaunty modern seaside-inspired schemes**
* **cream or sand carpet in twist-pile finish**
* **roller blinds or stripy curtains**
* **wooden venetian blinds**
* **brass or polished silver accessories**

colour tips

With a more limited colour palette, you may be concerned that your home will look bland if you stick rigidly to it in every room. But when you consider what an incredible range of blues there are to choose from, it soon becomes apparent how you can change the mood from airy and fresh to bold and bright, and even atmospherically moody, too. Traditional schemes generally work best when you restrict yourself to a choice of three or four sharply contrasting options from the palette. For example, one room could have **white walls**, a **red sofa** and a **blue armchair** with **sandy** carpet for a crisp family setting. While a dining room, for example, might suit **deep indigo walls** teamed with light wood (**sand** toned) furniture and smart **white linens** for a sophisticated and rich mood. Choosing a modern room scheme gives you even more flexibility as these rely on the use of lots of subtle layers of similar shades for a harmonious feel. Imagine **pale aqua walls** teamed with **white upholstery**, **turquoise curtains**, and **sky blue** and **cobalt blue cushions** and accessories for a perfect softly blended example.

contemporary coastal style

This alternative look is based on shades that more accurately reflect tropical climates, such as sky blue and aqua to echo the colours of brilliant sea and sky. White is added in healthy doses on walls and in linens and furniture, too, for a fresh, open-air feel, while neutral shades inspired by beaches and natural textures of rope and string also work beautifully. This is a great way to enhance newer properties and suits streamlined furniture designs in palest woods or distressed whitewashed paint effects for a sun-bleached feel.

- Think **tropical sea shades**

TONES LIKE:

chalk white	**azure**
string	**aquamarine**
soft yellow	**turquoise**
sky blue	

TEAM WITH

- **sun-bleached or distressed paint effects on furniture for a weathered look**
- **wooden window shutters or floaty voiles**
- **sanded or plain floorboards or natural textured floor-coverings**

WALLS

Bring the sense of sea, sand and sun into your home with interior walls that look a little weather-beaten or bleached from the sun. Rough plaster or sand texture paint effects and tongue-and-groove boarding to echo the look of shiplap panelling are just three great options.

Rustic textures work best to create an authentic beach feel, although classic blue and white nautical schemes and more contemporary coastal looks inspired by Caribbean seas work happily too with smooth walls on which the colour speaks for itself. Generally, patterned wall-coverings are best avoided, but if you want to emphasize a seaside theme with sailing boats or beach-hut motifs, or to add a tropical element with marine fish stencils, restrict yourself to borders or just one focal wall to stop the effect becoming too twee. Take your inspiration from sandy beaches for fine-textured paint effects, ship's panelling for ideas for using tongue-and-groove and even water itself for layered horizontal wavy stripes for a more adventurous look. The one time when smooth wall-coverings are perfectly acceptable is if you opt for a classic crisp navy and white nautical scheme, which suits a 'shipshape' and more polished look.

▸ **Sparkling aqua walls teamed with crisp white and fresh green create a marine-inspired scheme for a contemporary twist on coastal style. Aqua is warmer than sky blue, so it is perfect for rooms where light is lacking, if you are concerned that they may look too cold.**

▸▸ **Tongue-and-groove panelling is a brilliant choice for any room. Use it to dado height in a hallway, to decorate alcoves on either side of a fireplace in your living room or to cover one focal wall behind a bed. In a kitchen or bathroom it is ideal for covering almost the entire room, even the ceiling. Lime-wash, blue emulsion or wood stains are the best cover choices.**

◄ Wooden slatted open shelves hung at high level on walls suit the informality of coastal style, as well as providing invaluable storage space. Ideal for hallways, the shelves look best when left as natural, unvarnished wood or given a soft whitewashed finish. Store only boxed items to avoid anything tumbling on to your head. Look out for lightweight, cardboard storage boxes or galvanized metal tins to hide clutter, as both are in keeping with this style.

◄ Rough-plastered walls and emulsioned brickwork have a rustic quality that suits this style perfectly, so anyone with bumpy walls can at last see them as an advantage. There are many ways to add rough texture to walls but bear in mind that it may be time-consuming and costly to reverse the effect. Sand-textured paints like the one shown here are more subtle and can be painted on to lining paper, making them easier to remove.

▸ Create your own works of art by stretching canvas over batten frames and painting with acrylics. Here beach windbreaks provided inspiration for graphic striped images that add zing and focus to a plain wall.

FLOORS

There are an endless variety of different textured floorings – from sleek wood laminate to soft carpet – to suit coastal style so, whatever your budget, there are plenty of options to choose from. The only limiting factor is that coastal-style floorings are almost always neutral in tone, and your aim is to create a subdued finish underfoot rather than a full-on focal point.

Classic nautical blue and white schemes demand sophisticated finishes, such as sleek laminates or real wood in mid-toned or limed oak or birch for a sun-bleached finish. Neutral carpet in both twist and smooth-cut piles works beautifully, too. Vibrant seaside primary room schemes need greater contrast and suit richer, more contemporary wood tones, such as beech, and work beautifully with sand loop-pile or textured carpet. If your taste is for a more rustic, beachcomber theme or a tropical look, choose informal sanded or painted wooden floorboards or natural floor-coverings with a rugged weave. A two-tone chequerboard painted floor can look suitably seaside in the right colours and subtle stencilled motifs, such as shells and starfish, can make a pretty border on painted floorboards. Just avoid coordinating the look by stencilling walls in the same way as this will look over the top.

◀ **Laminate is the cheat's alternative if you find floorboards a little harsh and unforgiving underfoot. But be careful which wood tone you choose. Limed oak, pine, birch and mid-toned oak are all wonderfully authentic, while richer maple, cherry and deeper shades of mahogany seem just a bit too glossy and sophisticated to blend in.**

▶ **Cotton rugs are essential for softening white-painted floorboards or real-wood flooring and this delicate raised-weave rug with integral pattern is the ideal style choice. The clean white look is softened only by the motif to add textural interest without straying from the colour scheme.**

▾ Rougher-textured natural flooring is totally in keeping with the coastal theme. This rich honey shade calls to mind sandy beaches and makes a direct connection with the outdoors.

▴ Soft carpet in natural tones is ideal when teamed with blue walls and silver metals to echo the watery theme. Creamy shades are good in adults-only homes where freshness, light and an airy feel are important, but sand shades are perfect for a cosy mood and are more resilient when it comes to stains and general wear and tear.

◂ Bare floorboards sanded back for smoothness and painted in durable white emulsion are perfect for the coastal look. But for extra interest you could add a colourful chequered effect as shown here. Paint your base colour, leave to dry, mask off your pattern, fill in with another shade and remove the tape. Seal with a protective coat of satin floor varnish.

coastal style 209

FABRICS

To emulate the look of a coastal home successfully, you need to opt for durable, practical textured fabrics, almost all of them in plain-coloured finishes, although with the odd stripy pattern to add interest in a traditional scheme.

Choose a good mix and match of touchy–feely fabrics and you'll create a setting that entices you to relax – which is, of course, the whole point of this holiday-inspired style. Picture the rough richness of denim, the chunky knit of a fisherman's sweater, the crisp taut finish of a canvas sail and you have the key elements of traditional coastal-inspired fabrics firmly in mind. Brushed cottons and slubby linens work beautifully, as does hessian, which calls to mind the texture of nautical sacking and makes a surprisingly effective choice for curtaining. Contemporary rooms allow you to experiment with organzas and velvets for a rich, tropical feel and thick cord can look fabulous as upholstery. If pattern is important to you, it is wisest to stick to more classic schemes, which allow you to introduce jaunty anchor or boat motifs. Just remember to use such motifs in small amounts if you want to add character and charm. Overdosing on deliberately nautical imagery is the quickest way to a clichéd end result, which only ever works in a child's room.

◄ Striped fabrics in zingy primary tones make a wonderfully vibrant addition used in small doses, such as scatter cushions for a sofa.

▲ For a more deliberately seaside-themed look, choose vibrantly coloured fabrics with obvious nautical imagery to make a real statement. This fun bedlinen features almost childishly drawn motifs for a humorous scheme to suit adults who don't take themselves too seriously.

◄ Denim bedlinen is a brilliant choice if you want to interpret the beach look in a very modern, minimal way. It is also the case that men will generally prefer this look to a frilly, flouncy alternative.

KITCHEN

Small kitchens work particularly well with a coastal theme as they echo the authentic feel of a narrow ship's galley. But whatever size kitchen you have, the crisp blue, white and wood colour scheme starting point will make it a fresh, clean and pleasant room to work in.

Coastal-style kitchens and country kitchens share many similar ingredients because both aim to create an informal, rustic mood. So you need to concentrate on your colour choices and use of accessories to add that essential nautical touch. Limed-pine, whitewashed Shaker-style doors or indeed tongue-and-groove doors are all suitable. Avoid anything with a sophisticated gloss, such as laminate or Melamine, if you want an authentic result. Faking a wood-grain effect is a quick solution to dated doors, but you will need to invest in the correct paint and a wood-grain 'rocker'. Checked café-style curtains that hang from a half-height pole across the full width of the window make a pretty yet laid-back window treatment, although shutters work well, too. If you can, make space for a breakfast table. Choose untreated pine chairs with rush-covered seats for a traditional country look, or brushed silver for a modern marine scheme. A fisherman's-style lantern in brushed metal or brass hung over the table is the perfect accessory, as are wicker baskets, rattan vegetable racks and a slate noticeboard for scribbled chalk shopping lists or telephone messages.

▶ With their practical, informal feel, chunky cream or terracotta earthenware and this rich mid-toned wooden tray suit the kitchen scheme to perfection, wherever you decide to eat your breakfast.

▲ A fisherman's-style lamp in brass or silver is the ideal lighting choice to illuminate a kitchen dining table for informal suppers. Most high-street stores now stock great copies of this lighting classic.

◀ Tongue-and-groove walls and cupboard fronts are, strictly speaking, a country look but here, in fresh blue and white, they have a distinctly coastal quality. The striped pottery mimics Cornish tableware, while rustic wicker baskets on the cabinet top are reminiscent of lobster pots and nautical paraphernalia.

▲ Lanterns are ideal accessories for any room, hung from wall hooks or simply placed in groups on a table or mantelpiece. Brushed-silver or white enamel finishes are the best options. Avoid coloured glass, which suits more ethnic schemes.

◀ Transform a window with a charming handmade string and shell blind for an interesting focal point. It offers a modicum of privacy during the day without blocking out any light, but you will need a curtain at night.

kitchen essentials

✔ **white or pale-wood** Shaker-style or tongue-and-groove cupboard fronts
✔ **period-style** swan-necked kitchen tap
✔ **open shelving** such as informal cup-hooks
✔ **wooden venetian blind** or cotton roller blind

LIVING ROOM

Picture a perfect beach – golden sand, pale blue skies with fluffy white clouds and a fishing boat on the waves – and you have the basis for your scheme: a natural-toned carpet, palest blue or matt white walls and an ivory or hessian cotton roman blind echoing the texture of a sail.

Coastal style is about a pared-back approach that can deal with the wear and tear of everyday life. In fact, your furniture should look naturally aged, as if it has been sun-bleached over the years or knocked about in the course of your travels. Look for painted wicker sofas or spray paint rattan furniture yourself. To keep the holiday mood, hide the TV away under a canvas cover and hang an inspirational seascape as the perfect focal point instead. Softly draped muslin curtains add a romantic, dreamy feel to windows, particularly with informal tab-top headings. You may need to add heavier weight cotton curtains for winter but layering muslin over the top creates a similar feel. Pile an open fire with rough-hewn logs to turn a black hole into an eye-catching feature in summer. Or treat yourself to a cast-iron stove-style fire for a rustic flavour. There are some great electric fakes around.

▾ **Stripy or checked cushions in different shades of blue add a jaunty focus in seconds to a plain sofa or a bland bed. Look out for Aran knits too... the perfect echo of a snuggly fisherman's sweater.**

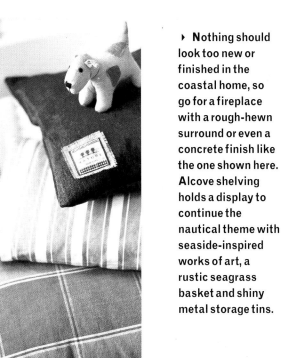

▸ **Nothing should look too new or finished in the coastal home, so go for a fireplace with a rough-hewn surround or even a concrete finish like the one shown here. Alcove shelving holds a display to continue the nautical theme with seaside-inspired works of art, a rustic seagrass basket and shiny metal storage tins.**

‣ **Checked blue and white tableware on a whitewashed tray provides an instant nautical feel to enhance your holiday mood as you take afternoon tea.**

✔ **wickerwork or rattan** seating in natural or white-painted finishes

✔ **lime-washed furniture**, including a multi-drawered chest or bookcase

✔ **unusual coffee table**, such as merchant's chest or battered pale leather suitcase

✔ **plate rack** or high-level shelf

✔ **linen- or ivory-coloured cotton** tab-top curtains or roman blind

✔ **seascape prints** or photographs

◂ **The predominantly chalk and sail-white colour scheme keeps this living room bright, airy and open – from the white-painted wicker sofa to the sheer muslin curtains at the windows. Touches of navy blue and primary red and a large variety of different textures prevent the overall result looking too stark and bland.**

◂ **Pebble-themed accessories such as this smooth rock-based lamp are ideal for contemporary coastal style. It is thoughtful details like these that really cement your room scheme.**

BEDROOM

Lime-washed furniture is a great way to add an instant coastal theme to a bedroom. Unlike white-painted pieces that suit country style, this finish makes the most of the wood grain and echoes beachcomber finds of weathered sun-bleached timbers.

Always opt for freestanding pieces – preferably unmatching – for a suitably relaxed, informal mood. When it comes to your bed, a metal or wooden bedstead in white or unfinished pine is the best choice, although updating a divan with a linen- or canvas-covered headboard can work wonders, too. Look out for bedlinen in large blue and white checks or stripes, in pure white or even in denim effect, to make reference to hardy seafaring fishermen's attire. Quirky touches like battered leather suitcases used as under-bed storage or piled up for bedside tables, and lanterns hung from hooks on the wall all add personality to the scheme. In a guest room, a peg rail on a wall or the back of the door makes wonderful instant storage for overnight clothes. Plus, if you have space, an enamel freestanding washstand or ceramic bowl and jug on top of a chest of drawers add a charming feature and

bedroom **essentials**

- ✔ **white-painted** or pine bedstead
- ✔ **lime-washed** chest of drawers
- ✔ **freestanding** white-painted wardrobe
- ✔ **rattan** or wicker linen chest or occasional chair
- ✔ **fisherman's-style** ceiling light
- ✔ **natural-toned** texture-woven carpet

echo the washing facilities on-board old steamers. Hessian roman blinds add a rugged finish to windows, then complete the look with silvery accessories such as an antique-style alarm clock.

▾ **Little touches make all the difference in bringing a nautical theme to life. This wooden lamp base has been whitewashed, while the picture frame has been given a distressed paint effect to make it look sun bleached and peeling.**

▸ **Create a sense of seaside breezes with delicate, fresh blue and white checked voile floating at your open window. A white-emulsioned junk-shop dining chair and a wooden model boat complete the look.**

▾ This soft and cosy bedroom scheme takes its modern seaside mood not from overtly nautical images but from a modern, crisp use of strong blue walls and touches of white and natural sandy tones for floors, bedlinen and blinds. A slubby neutral linen makes the ideal fabric choice for a padded headboard and for streamlined blinds that echo the look of ship's sails at the windows. The modern mobile above the bed suggests a subliminal connection with rain and water for a coastal mood.

▸ A white-painted wrought-iron daybed makes a wonderful choice for a guest bedroom, while doubling up as a sofa in a regularly used living space. Here crisp blue and white checked bedlinen shows that bold, modern fabrics suit the coastal theme, too.

BATHROOM

Because of its direct relationship with water, this is the one room where you really can go overboard on nautical style for a dramatic themed look if you want. Experiment with stencilled imagery on walls and quirky accessories such as model boats for fun.

Tongue-and-groove wall panelling will add a rustic beach feel and is great for disguising bumpy walls or creating a stylish bath panel, although you will need to protect the wood from water splashes and humidity with two or three coats of yacht varnish. If you do opt for this, fix the panelling on battens that sit proud of the wall by at least 7.5cm (3in) and you will also make a shelf for displaying seaside accessories like shells and starfish, and candles, as well as all your toiletries. A port-hole mirror is another way of giving a nautical flavour, and if your bathroom door is thick enough, consider adding a coordinating frosted glass port-hole to let in more light and emphasize the theme. In family homes decorating walls with seaside murals can be fun. Paint beach huts, seagulls, sandcastles and so on, then hang real buckets and spades on the walls as storage for toiletries. A sandy-coloured carpet and a cloudy-sky ceiling complete the scene.

bathroom **essentials**

- ✔ **roll-top bath**
- ✔ **tongue-and-groove** wall panelling with display/storage shelf
- ✔ **period-style** pedestal basin
- ✔ **period-style** bath/shower mixer tap
- ✔ **wood-effect** vinyl flooring or sanded varnished floorboards
- ✔ **peg rail** or back-of-door hooks

▾ **Subtle rope-edge detailing gives this basin a nautical twist and is ideally suited to period-style homes and cottages. Almost every sanitary ware manufacturer has something similar in its range.**

▸ **A roller blind in vibrant aqua adds a sharp, fresh contrast to sky blue in this bathroom and shows how the coastal theme can be extended to include looks inspired by Caribbean seas as well as less sun-drenched places.**

◀ **A** chalky white and wood colour scheme sets the perfect mood for a coastal-style bathroom. Here a freestanding roll-top bath, teamed with rough-painted whitewashed furniture and sanded, varnished floorboards create an informal open-plan feel; while an opaque blind with a crisp, nautical motif creates an essential note of prettiness to avoid blandness in an otherwise one-colour room.

▼ **Q**uirky nautical stencils or stamped motifs add character and personality. Here a charming beach-hut stamp has been used to create a subtle border trim above tongue-and-groove panelling. **K**ids will love to help with this, so look out for fish, starfish, bucket and spade, and even bobbing boat motifs and have a go.

index

acknowledgements

Allders /'from a selection of lamps at Allders' 215 bottom right.

Amtico /www.amtico.com (stockists tel: +44 (0)800 667 766) 68 centre right, 208 left.

Anaglypta /(stockists tel: +44 (0)1254 704 951) 27 bottom left, 207 top.

Andrew Martin /(tel: +44 (0)20 7225 5103) 103 top right, 168 right.

And So To Bed /www.andsotobed.co.uk (tel: +44 (0)808 144 4343) 23 left, 26 left, 36 right, 37 bottom right.

Art Room /www.artroom.com (orderline: +44 (0)870 242 7733) 174, 175 bottom right, 176–177 centre.

Laura Ashley /'© Laura Ashley Limited 2002' 20, 21, 22, 31 left, 31 bottom right, 37 top, 42, 51 bottom right, 54–55 centre, 59 top right, 101, 109 top, 114 bottom, 115 top right, 116 bottom right, 116 bottom left, 117 main, 217 main.

Bathaus /92 Brompton Road, Knightsbridge, London, SW3 1ER, UK (tel: +44 (0)20 7225 7620) 79 bottom right, 99 top left.

Bedeck Bedlinen /www.bedeckhome.com (tel: +44 (0)845 603 0861) 77 top left.

British Wool Marketing Board /Russell Sadur Photography 209 top right.

Nina Campbell /'by Nina Campbell for Osborne & Little' /www.osborneandlittle.com (stockists tel: +44 (0)20 7352 1456) 87 top left, 171 bottom.

Jane Churchill /(stockists tel: +44 (0)20 8877 6400) 216 right.

Colony Gift Corporation Ltd /(stockists tel: +44 (0)1229 461 111) 176 left.

Coloroll /bedlinen from Coloroll range 2001. For further details please visit www.coloroll.co.uk 77 main.

Corian /www.corian.co.uk (tel: +44 (0)800 962 116) 33 top right, 113 bottom right.

The Cotswold Company /www.cotswoldco.com (stockists tel: +44 (0)870 600 3436) 136 right.

Courts /www.courts.co.uk (tel: +44 (0)800 600 900) 74 bottom centre, 128 right.

Crabtree & Evelyn Ltd /www.crabtree-evelyn.co.uk (stockists tel: +44 (0)20 7603 1611) 162.

Crown Paints /www.crownpaint.co.uk (advice tel: +44 (0)1254 704 951) 9, 15 top, 26 right, 34 right, 49 bottom left, 63 top right, 66 bottom left, 71 bottom right, 126 right, 127 top left, 206 left, 207 bottom left, 218 right.

Crown Imperial /(stockists tel: +44 (0)1227 74 24 24) 72 bottom left.

Crowson Fabrics /(stockists tel: +44 (0)1825 761 055) 34 left, 97 left, 171 top right .

Crucial Trading Ltd /(stockists tel: +44 (0)1562 820 006) 149 bottom left, 168 left.

Dolomite /www.dolomite-bathrooms.com (stockists tel: +44 (0)800 138 0922) 78.

Dolphin Bathrooms /www.dolphinbathrooms.com (stockists tel: +44 (0)800 626 717) 38–39 centre.

Dorma /www.dormahome.com (stockists tel: +44 (0)161 251 4400) 1, 12, 91 top right.

Dulux /www.dulux.co.uk (tel: +44 (0)1753 550 555) 10, 86 left, 87 bottom, 142, 143 centre left, 148, 167 right, 172 right, 179 left, 196–197 centre, 214 right.

Early's of Whitney /(stockists tel: +44 (0)870 523 9633) 131 bottom.

Elgin & Hall /www.elgin.co.uk (stockists tel: +44 (0)1667 450 100) 102, 118–119 centre, 119 top left, 119 bottom right.

The English Stamp Company /www.englishstamp.com (stockists: +44 (0)1929 439 117) 46 right, 166 left, 219 bottom right.

Fired Earth /www.firedearth.com (stockists tel: +44 (0)1295 814 300) 13, 32 right, 48 left, 88 right, 106 top right, 107 top right, 108 bottom left, 109 bottom right, 118 bottom centre, 126 left, 128 left, 129 bottom left, 189 right.

Graham & Brown /www.grahambrown.com (stockists tel: +44 (0)800 328 8452) 67 bottom right.

Grange /(stockist tel: +44 (0)20 7935 7000) 129 top, 132–133 bottom centre, 137 top.

H&R Johnson /www.johnson-tiles.com (tel: +44 (0)1782 575575) 112 bottom left.

Harlequin Fabrics and Wallcoverings Ltd /(tel: +44 (0)1509 225 000) 28 left.

Heritage Bathrooms PLC. /www.heritagebathrooms.com (stockists tel: +44 (0)117 953 5000) 159 main.

The Holding Company /www.theholdingcompany.co.uk (stockists tel: +44 (0)20 8445 2888) 98 top.

Homelux /pictures supplied courtesy of Homelux 186 right.

Ideal Standard Ltd /www.ideal-standard.co.uk (Tel: +44 (0)800 590 311) 89 top right, 138 bottom left.

IKEA UK /www.IKEA.co.uk (stockists tel: +44 (0)20 8208 5600) 58, 75 top right, 92 left, 93 top, 152 bottom left, 153 main.

The Interior Archive /Tim Beddow/ Designer: Kathryn Ireland 6, 7, 209 bottom, /Simon Brown/ Designer: Peter Sheppard 112 bottom right, 113 main, /Fritz von der Schulenburg/ Designer: Jed Johnson 146 left, /Fritz von der Schulenburg/ Designer: Mimmi O'Connell 122, 178 right.

The Iron Bed Company /www.ironbed.com (stockists tel: +44 (0)1243 578 888) 129 bottom right, 137 bottom left.

Jewel Fabrics and Wallcoverings /(stockists tel: +44 (0)1509 225 000) 16 centre right, 69 top left.

KA International /www.ka-international.com (tel: +44 (0)20 7584 7352) 23 right, 120 left, 121, 123 right, 131 top left, 133 bottom right, 151 top, 151 bottom left.

Kahlfloor /(stockists tel: +44 (0)151 549 0101) 88 left.

Kersaint Cobb /(stockists tel: +44 (0)1675 430 430/ brochure hotline: +44 (0)800 028 5371) 89 top left.

Luxaflex /Luxaflex blinds can be found at Bentalls, Allders and around 1800 independent furnishing stores. 2–3, 16 bottom right, 63 top left, 73 top right.

Magnet /www.magnet.co.uk (stockists tel: +44 (0)800 192 192) 33 main picture 36 left, 76 bottom right, 99 bottom left, 203 top, 213 main.

Ray Main /Mainstream 14 top, 47 top left, 166 right, 169 top left, 193 top.

Manhattan Showers /www.manhattanshowers.co.uk (Tel: +44 (0)1282 605 000) 38 left.

Maui Waui Design /(tel: +44 (0)1728 660 238/ Stephen Wolfenden) 33 bottom right.

McCord /www.emccord.com (stockists tel: +44 (0)870 908 7005) 111 bottom left, 175 top right, 176 bottom right.

MFI /www.mfi.co.uk (stockist tel: +44 (0)870 609 5555) 32 left, 149 bottom right, 188, 203 bottom.

MK Electric /www.mkelectric.co.uk (stockists tel: +44 (0)1268 563 370) 212 top right.

Monkwell Fabrics /www.monkwell.com (tel: +44 (0)1202 752 944) 55 top right, 111 top.

Monsoon /www.monsoon.co.uk (stockists tel: +44 (0)7313 3000) 15 bottom.

Narratives /Jan Baldwin 199 top left, /Peter Dixon /Design by A & M Shaw 14 bottom, 67 top.

The National Magazine Company Limited 16 centre left, 17 centre left, 17 centre right, 40, 41, 43 Top, 43 bottom, 47 bottom left, 51 top, 52 top, 52 bottom, 53 left, 53 right, 53 bottom right, 54 left, 55 bottom right, 56 left, 56 right, 57 top, 57 bottom right, 57 bottom left, 59 top left, 59 bottom left, 62, 66 right, 81, 83 top, 83 bottom, 86 right, 87 top right, 91 top left, 93 bottom right, 94 top, 94 bottom right, 95 top left, 95 bottom, 96 left, 96 bottom right, 107 bottom, 111 bottom right, 113 top right, 115 main, 115 bottom right, 117 bottom right, 127 right, 131 top right, 133 top left, 134 bottom right, 134 bottom left, 135 top, 135 bottom, 136 left, 143 top right, 146 right, 147 bottom, 152 bottom right, 153 top right, 154 left, 156 top right, 156 bottom right, 157 top left, 157 top right, 158 left, 174 left, 174–175 centre, 177 bottom, 178 left, 179 right, 180, 181, 182, 183 top, 187 top left, 189 bottom left, 191 top, 191 bottom left, 194 left, 194 right, 194 centre, 195 top left, 195 bottom, 198 right, 200, 201, 202, 206 right, 207 bottom right, 209 top left, 211 top left, 211 top right, 212 bottom left, 213 centre right, 213 bottom left, 214 left, 214–215 main picture, 215 top, 216 left, 217 top right.

Natural Flooring Direct /(stockists tel: +44 (0)800 454 721) 29 top left.

New House Textiles /www.newhousetextiles.co.uk (stockists tel: +44 (0)1989 740 684) 76 bottom left.

Next /www.next.co.uk /From the Next Home Collection Autumn/ Winter 2001 (For details of the Next Directory tel: +44 (0)845 600 7000) 68 bottom left, 99 bottom right, 114 top, 172 left, 211 bottom.

Nice Irma's /www.niceirma.com (stockists tel: +44 (0)20 8343 9766) 173 bottom right.

Nordic Style Ltd /www.nordicstyle.com (stockists tel: +44 (0)20 7351 1755) 140, 141, 147 top left, 151 bottom right, 154 right, 154 centre, 155 main, 157 main

Novatec /(stockists tel: +44 (0)1843 850 666) 219 main.

Ocean Home Shopping /www.oceanuk.com (orderline: +44 (0)870 242 6283) 158 right, 159 top left.

Octopus Publishing Group Limited /Tom Mannion 4, 5, 16 top right, 69 top right, 71 bottom left, 72 bottom right, 73 bottom right, 74–75 centre, 138 top right, /Peter Myers 173 left, /William Reavell 92 right, /Polly Wreford 39 top right, 138 bottom right, 163 Top, 167 top left, /Mel Yates 167 bottom left, 177 top right.

The Original Seagrass Co. /www.original-seagrass.co.uk (tel: +44 (0)1588 673 666) 49 bottom right.

Original Style Ltd /www.originalstyle.com (stockists tel: +44 (0)1392 474 058) 29 right.

The Pier /www.pier.co.uk (tel: +44 (0)845 609 1234) 16 bottom left, 59 bottom right , 97 top right, 97 bottom right, 133 top right, 160, 161, 171 top left.

Porcelanosa /(stockists tel: +44 (0)800 915 4000) 60, 61, 67 bottom left, 109 bottom left, 123 left, 127 bottom, 132 left.

Qualitas 39 bottom right.

Ronseal /www.ronseal.co.uk (tel: +44 (0)114 2409 469) 89 bottom.

Royal Doulton Bathrooms /www.royaldoultonbathrooms.com (stockists tel: +44 (0)1270 879 777) 69 bottom, 79 top, 169 top right, 199 bottom right.

Samuel Heath & Sons PLC /www.samuel-heath.com (tel: +44 (0)121 766 4200) 39 top left.

Sanderson /www.sanderson-uk.com (tel: +44 (0)1895 830 044) 16 top left, 27 top left, 31 top right, 35 top, 46 left, 82, 106 bottom left.

Shaker /www.shaker.co.uk (tel: +44 (0)20 7935 9461) 17 top, 183 centre, 186 left, 187 top right, 187 bottom right, 191 right, 192 left, 192 right, 193 bottom, 196 left, 197 top right, 197 bottom right, 198 left, 199 top right.

Stoddard /www.stoddardcarpets.com (tel: +44 (0)800 027 4888) 28 right.

Stonell Ltd /(tel: +44 (0)1892 833 500) 49 top.

Stoneham Opticolour /from the Avant Garde collection/ www.stoneham-kitchens.co.uk 73 main.

Swish /(stockists tel: +44 (0)500 008 572) 93 bottom left, 147 top right, 218 left.

The Tintawn Weaving Co. /simply natural in 100% pure wool pile 6 ply-yarn (tel: +44 (0)1372 363 393) 189 top left.

Twyford Bathrooms /www.twyfordbathrooms.com (stockists tel: +44 (0)1270 879 777) 163 bottom.

Vantona /(stockist tel: +44 (0)161 251 1500) 91 bottom left.

Villeroy & Boch /www.villeroy-boch.com (stockists tel: +44 (0)20 8871 4028) 79 bottom left, 98 bottom, 139 top, 139 bottom.

Vitra /www.vitrauk.com (tel: +44 (0)1235 820 400) 48 right.

The White Company /www.thewhiteco.com (tel: +44 (0)870 160 1610) 51 bottom left, 71 top, 119 top right, 208 right.

Wickes /www.wickes.co.uk (for further information please call the helpline on +44 (0)500 300 328) 47 right.

Mark Wilkinson Furniture /The Metro Kitchen – Designed by Mark Wilkinson/ www.mwf.com (tel: +44 (0)1380 850 004) 103 bottom left.

Wilman Interiors /www.wilman.co.uk 8, 11, 27 right, 29 bottom left, 35 bottom left, 100, 107 top left, 155 top right.

Wood Bros (Furniture) Ltd /www.look2000.co.uk (stockists tel: +44 (0)1920 469 241) 75 bottom right

Wood Floor Studio /www.woodfloorstudio.com (stockists tel: +44 (0)800 214 393) 149 top.

Woodward Grosvenor /Barley 30/3035 from the Harvester range. (product information: +44 (0)800 526 696) 169 bottom left.

Wools of New Zealand /made by Ryalux Carpets Tel: +44 (0)800 163 632/ www.woolsnz.com 108 top right.

Executive Editor **Anna Southgate**
Editor **Sharon Ashman**
Senior Designer **Rozelle Bentheim**
Book Designer **Jo Bennett**
Designer **Lisa Tai**
Senior Picture Researcher **Zoë Holtermann**
Senior Production Controller **Jo Sim**
Index **Indexing Specialists**